Pragmatic Project Management

Five Scalable Steps to Success

Pragmatic Project Management

Five Scalable Steps to Success

David Pratt, PMP

MANAGEMENTCONCEPTS

MANAGEMENTCONCEPTS
8230 Leesburg Pike, Suite 800
Vienna, VA 22182
(703) 790-9595
Fax: (703) 790-1371
www.managementconcepts.com

Printed in the United States of America

Library of Congress Cataloging-in-Publication Data

Pratt, David, 1954-
Pragmatic project management : five scalable steps to success / David Pratt.
p. cm.
ISBN 978-1-56726-274-2
1. Project management. I. Title.
HD69.P75P66 2010
658.4'04--dc22

2009048305

10 9 8 7 6 5 4 3 2 1

About the Author

David Pratt, PMP, has more than 20 years' experience managing projects of all types and sizes in both the public and private sectors. He is currently the principal of DHP Project Services, an IT project management consulting firm.

Mr. Pratt has taught undergraduate- and graduate-level business courses in the United States and in China. He currently teaches courses in project management at the South Puget Sound Community College in Lacey, Washington, where he helped design the project management certificate program.

A retired military officer and hospital administrator, Mr. Pratt holds master's degrees in management (Webster University) and hospital administration (Baylor University) and a bachelor's degree in psychology (Washington State University). He has authored more than 60 articles and is a columnist for a weekly regional newspaper.

Mr. Pratt is a frequent conference speaker on topics including change management, leadership, innovation, and motivation. He is a member of numerous service and professional groups, including Lions Clubs International, the Project Management Institute, and the Military Officers Association of America.

To Jacqueline, who has tolerated my need to create through project management and writing for so many years. Also, to my past employer Kent Meisner, who once said that he would never hire a project manager who hadn't participated on a failed project at least once. Those people, Kent suggested, have learned why managing projects carefully is so important.

Contents

Preface

Imagine starting a new job and feeling eager to prove your capabilities. One day your boss approaches you with a smile and says, "I've got a project for you." Your heart races. You have never managed a project before and have had only a little project management training. If you succeed, you will establish yourself in the company as a capable project manager, but if you fail....

Whether you are an experienced project manager or a first-timer with little or no training, this scenario is probably all too familiar. On one hand, a new project offers a chance to excel and deliver value to the organization. On the other hand, project management is hard and fraught with risk.

Project management is a complex discipline, replete with challenges and potential rewards. Unfortunately, too many projects struggle and fail right out of the door. The Standish Group, a major source of project management research and best-practice information, predicts that only 35 percent of all projects will succeed; another 46 percent will finish "challenged" (i.e., late, over budget, or with reduced functionality); and 19 percent will fail outright. The Standish Group identifies numerous factors that contribute to project success, including:

- Swift, decisive decision-making
- Clear business objectives
- Clear project vision
- Project management expertise
- Skilled project team resources
- A methodology tailored to the specific needs of the project
- The right tools, used correctly.[1]

---

[1] The Standish Group International, *CHAOS Summary 2009: The 10 Laws of CHAOS* (Boston: The Standish Group International, Inc., 2009), pp. 1–3.

While the Standish Group study focuses on IT projects, it is not difficult to see how its conclusions can be applied to projects across all industries.

For new and experienced project managers alike, it is hard to know how to approach a project. Is it best to pick a specific methodology and systematically march through it from beginning to end, regardless of the project's size or complexity? Or should project managers do something less rigorous and hope for the best? Is there enough time or funds to develop extensive plans, or can the effort be tailored to meet specific project needs?

If you have been in the project management profession for a while, you are probably aware of the plethora of methodologies and tools available to help manage projects. Perhaps you have used some of these tools or applied a few of the methodologies. Based on your past project management successes and failures, which of those tools and methodologies really mattered?

Pragmatic project management (PM) answers these questions. The pragmatic PM approach was developed in response to a survey of senior public- and private-sector project managers who were asked to identify the most common project management tools and approaches they relied upon to deliver successful projects. Their responses were consistent in every case:

- Write the project charter. Describe project objectives clearly and in sufficient detail.
- Build the project team. Define critical roles, responsibilities, and communication methods.
- Plan the project. Identify the project work and plan its order of completion in sufficient detail to understand how the project will move from initiation to successful delivery.
- Manage project issues. Address matters straying from the project plan as they arise.
- Track and report project progress. Keep the project on target by identifying its progress against the project plan and accounting for any differences. Report project status to the project sponsor, project team, and other stakeholders.

These responses form the basis behind pragmatic PM—a simple, practical, and scalable model that works. Pragmatic PM consists of five essential elements: the project charter, the project team, the project plan, project issue management, and project status tracking and reporting. Each element can be scaled to meet a project's particular size and complexity.

When a project schedule is tight, project managers often find themselves with too little time to adequately plan and organize their projects. The key is to determine the minimum amount of project management effort needed to deliver the maximum benefit for the project. Small projects require only a little effort, and the burden of that effort does not have to be overwhelming. For medium-sized and large projects, management efforts can be expanded or scaled to meet project needs. Once the project manager clearly identifies a project's needs, he or she can align those needs with a simple, straightforward process. This is what pragmatic PM is all about.

This book begins with a chapter on sizing and scaling and follows with chapters on each of the five essential elements of pragmatic project management. At the end of each of the chapters is a checklist for that element. Use the checklists as you plan and execute projects to maximize the pragmatic PM approach.

Each chapter also contains various rules of pragmatic PM, which are combined in a comprehensive list at the end of the book. These rules will remind you of important things to consider when managing projects.

Project management is one of the most challenging and rewarding jobs in the business world. At its most basic level, project management is about creating something new, whether it is a new building, computer system, or volunteer management program. But the practice is not simple or easy; it requires a systematic approach and discipline. I hope the pragmatic PM approach I offer in this book will help guide you toward consistent project management success.

David Pratt
Yelm, Washington

Acknowledgments

This book would not have been possible without the suggestions, advice, and support provided by a number of people. First and foremost among them is my wife, who patiently tolerated the many days I spent at the keyboard. Second is my primary reader, Sharon Hoback, who offered insightful suggestions and tactful criticism.

Within my professional circle, I must thank the many project managers who have, through our numerous discussions about project management, made contributions to my understanding of the discipline. They include Gil Dean, Glenn Briskin, Herb Widuschek, Mary Schwartz, Kent Meisner, Dave Taylor, and Sharon Sikes.

I would like to also thank the many project management students I have instructed over the years at Embry-Riddle Aeronautical University and South Puget Sound Community College, whose questions and challenges have kept my PM knowledge sharp over the years.

Finally, I would like to extend my appreciation to Myra Strauss, Courtney Chiaparas, and the crew at Management Concepts for making the journey from idea to publication such a great trip.

Introduction

Gather a group of project managers together in a room and the war stories flow without prompting. Tales abound of the big project that got away or of snatching victory from the teeth of overwhelming risk. There is no better way to gather lessons learned and insight into the mysteries, failures, and successes of the project management world than from seasoned veterans.

Not all veterans, however, have sterling records or have successfully sorted out the best PM practices for all types of projects. Many project managers are purists: They relentlessly apply a strict methodology to each project from its charter to its closeout. They leave no plan unwritten, defining every task to a minute level of detail, regardless of whether the task is easy or hard and no matter how much the excessive planning costs the project.

Forcing all projects into the same detailed framework regardless of actual need is a common problem. With project failure rates high, there can be a tendency to overreact through excessive planning, risk avoidance, and so on, which can all drive a project's budget and schedule into the ground.

At the other end of the PM spectrum are those who feel that even the most basic project management techniques are a waste of time, a needless bureaucracy impeding project objectives. I recall an invitation from a large state agency to participate in a project it was preparing to launch. I agreed to begin work on the project immediately and asked the project sponsor to forward any existing project documentation. That way, I told him, I could hit the ground running when I wrote the project's charter.

The project sponsor responded by saying that the agency did not ascribe to "PM bureaucracy" because there was too much work to do and too little time to do it, and it simply got in the way of progress.

I decided to turn down the project because I did not think my approach would fit very well with the agency's approach to projects. The project charter identifies the project's objectives, key milestones, roles, responsibilities, budget, management approach, and more; without it, the project is not likely to succeed. To be successful, every project needs to incorporate certain essential elements, regardless of its size and complexity.

Somewhere between over-relying on project management dogma and rejecting all project management is the perfect approach for every project. Project managers must identify among the numerous PM tools and techniques those that are most appropriate for each project. This is the essence of pragmatic PM.

The pragmatic PM approach is simple and straightforward:

1. Always begin with the five essential elements of pragmatic PM (the project charter, the project team, the project plan, project issue management, and project status tracking and reporting), regardless of project size and complexity.
2. Scale your application of the five essential elements to meet the project's size and complexity.

The essence of pragmatic PM is using minimum effort to achieve maximum project gain. For small projects, apply relatively less project management. For large projects, apply relatively more project management. Figure I-1 offers a basic depiction of the pragmatic PM scaling model.

The five essential elements form the backbone of pragmatic PM. Figure I-2 shows how the elements fit together to manage a project from its initial charter to its completion.

WRITING THE PROJECT CHARTER

Having a good description of the project at the outset is essential to project success. Simply put, without a description of even the most

Figure I-1 The Pragmatic Project Management Scaling Model

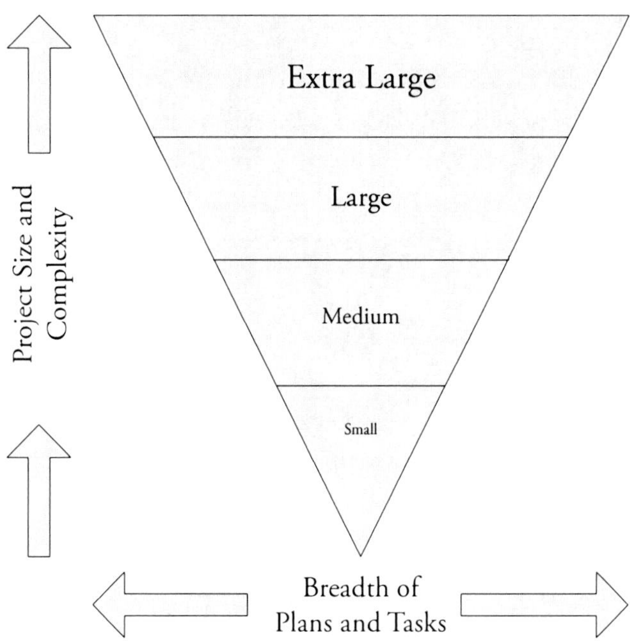

Figure I-2 The Five Essential Elements of Pragmatic Project Management

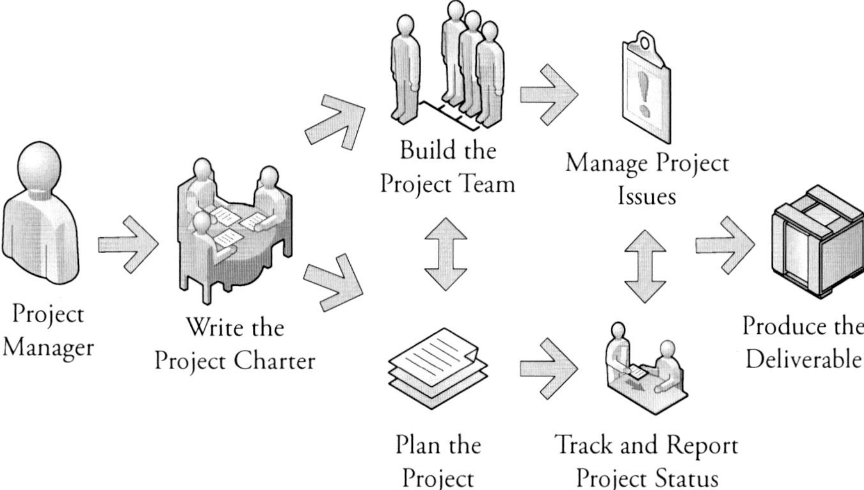

simple aspects of the project, it will be difficult to complete the project efficiently and successfully.

If the nature of the product or service the project is meant to deliver is unknown, the project will lack a necessary focus. Knowing the project sponsor's objectives and the value the sponsor expects the project to deliver is essential when it comes to directing the project toward success. A good project charter clarifies these points and more.

BUILDING THE PROJECT TEAM

Once the project has been reasonably described, the project manager is ready to assemble a talented, appropriately sized project team. One axiom of project management is that the people who do the work should do the planning, too. More minds on a problem generally results in a better solution. Projects are problem-solving exercises where the end product or service is the solution, so having a good team whose members can cooperate to develop an appropriate solution can make all the difference.

A project team should consist of the minimum number of skill sets necessary to satisfy the project's objectives, as described in the project charter. For a very small project, the team might be just two or three people. For large, complex projects, the number can vary from ten to 50 people or more. Focus on scaling the team to meet the project's needs: no more, no less.

PLANNING THE PROJECT

Project plans, like project charters, can be as brief or as extensive as necessary. The plan is essentially a project schedule that can be documented simply as a list of tasks and dates or developed as an integrated project plan using a more elaborate tool like Microsoft Project. As with the project charter, the plan must be documented formally, ensuring its preservation over time and in the event of project personnel changes.

MANAGING PROJECT ISSUES

Once the charter is written, the team assembled, and the project planned, the real work begins. The project manager is responsible for managing the team as it executes the plan and addressing any issues that arise. Unmanaged issues can evolve into risks and changes to project scope, which may require a project team to reassess its budget and schedule requirements. Sometimes issues are small and can be resolved simply. Other issues require escalation above the project manager to the project sponsor.

As with the project charter, project team, and project plan, project issue management varies depending on the needs of the project. On small projects with a lean team, issues can generally be handled effectively in an informal environment. Large or complex projects with big teams and numerous stakeholders may require a more formal issue management process involving detailed risk management and integrated change-control processes.

Regardless of how the project team scales its approach to issue management, it should always pay special attention to issues affecting project scope, schedule, or cost. An issue that affects one of these factors will affect each of the others. These issues impact the project at its most fundamental level.

TRACKING AND REPORTING PROJECT STATUS

Project status tracking and reporting is the final essential element of pragmatic project management. Stepping back from the day-to-day management of the project, project managers assess the project's status against schedule, scope, and cost expectations outlined in the project plan, determine how well things are going, and make adjustments as necessary.

Project status reports are often provided to the project sponsor and other stakeholders. In this sense, the status report is an excellent communications tool. The project manager can present the report either in a formal, written format for large, complex projects or more informally for small projects.

BRINGING IT ALL TOGETHER

This book is meant to help readers put the five essential elements of pragmatic PM together to deliver a successful project. Scaling the application of the elements to the specific needs of each project is the key to success. Beginning with a chapter on sizing projects and adjusting project management to scale and following with chapters that each address an essential element of pragmatic PM, this book provides a practical, accessible approach that anyone can use for any type of project.

Chapter 1

Sizing the Project and Adjusting Project Management to Scale

Every project is unique. Some projects are small; others are large. Some are relatively inexpensive and some cost a fortune. Some projects are simple, straightforward, predictable, and well understood; others are highly complex and risky. Each project requires a different level of project management; applying the same amount of attention, resources, and documentation to each project is typically wasteful. Despite this, many organizations and project managers apply project management dogmatically without deviation, instead of scaling efforts appropriately.

The goal of pragmatic project management is to determine the minimum amount of project management effort needed to deliver the maximum benefit for the project. To do this, the project must first be sized according to its specific characteristics.

SIZING THE PROJECT

All projects, regardless of cost, size, complexity, and risk, progress through a standard project lifecycle that includes initial, intermediate, and final phases. The initial phase typically includes the business idea, the project charter, the project team, and the project scope statement. The intermediate phase typically includes the project plan, project baselines, project execution, and project progress tracking and reporting. The final phase includes project approval and closeout.

Pragmatic PM Rule #1: All projects move through a standard, predictable project lifecycle.

The first effort at sizing a project generally takes place early in the initial phase—when the project is simply an undeveloped business idea or concept. At this point, the organization may have only limited information about the project, and it may have to base its initial understanding of the project on assumptions or on historical data from analogous projects. Despite the limited amount of information, the organization should be able to make an initial estimation of the project's relative size, complexity, cost, risk, and organizational impact. Each of these factors will have an effect on project feasibility and, subsequently, the project team's approach.

Pragmatic PM Rule #2: Despite the limited amount of information available during the initial phase of the project lifecycle, the sponsoring organization should be able to make an initial estimation of the project's relative size, complexity, cost, risk, and organizational impact.

The project sizing matrix is a good tool to use in assessing the relative size of a project (Figure 1-1). This tool incorporates major factors affecting project size, including project cost, complexity (the estimated number of tasks), anticipated risk level, and organizational impact.

Cost estimates in the initial phase of the project lifecycle will be only high-level estimates. As the project evolves through the project lifecycle and the project team refines project objectives, requirements, and resource estimates, cost estimates will become more exact, and the project's true size will become more clear.

Similarly, project complexity estimates in the initial phase will be based only on assumptions about how much work—and what kind of work—the project will entail.

Figure 1-1 The Project Sizing Matrix

Project	Anticipated Cost	Anticipated Complexity	Anticipated Risk	Organizational Impact
Very small project	$25K to $50K	Few tasks	Low risk	One organization or department
Small project	$50K to $100K	< 100 tasks	Low risk	One organization or department
Medium project	$100K to $1M	100 to 500 tasks	Low-to-medium risk	Multiple organizations or multiple departments within one organization
Large project	> $1M	Over 500 tasks	High risk	Multiple organizations or multiple departments within one organization

The project manager's assessment of risk must be consistent with what the sponsoring organization constitutes a high, medium, or low risk. Some organizations, for example, define high-risk projects as those with at least a 40 percent probability of failure. For others, a ten percent probability of project failure is considered high-risk.

When a project has an impact across organizational boundaries, the associated challenges and considerations for the project sponsor, PM, and project team increase proportionally. Organizational cultures, management styles, strategies, goals, and objectives can differ markedly from one organization to another and from one department to another within a single organization. In these cases, the project sponsor and PM must spend a great deal of time working with stakeholders from each organization or department to ensure project deliverables meet the needs of all stakeholders. Political considerations in these cases will typically require a more conscientious, sophisticated project approach.

Few projects land exactly within the parameters identified by the project sizing matrix. Consider, for example, a project estimated to cost $100,000, to include 100 tasks, and to have a relatively low level of risk. According to the project sizing matrix, that project would typically be considered small. But what if that project impacts two organizations, including the project sponsor's agency? Would the project still be considered small? In this case, because many of the indices are right on the border of being typical for medium-sized projects, and because there is a significant political aspect to the project impacting multiple organizations, the PM should probably approach this as a medium-sized project.

SCALING THE WORK

After sizing the project during the initial phase of the project lifecycle, the next step is to tailor the pragmatic PM approach to meet the needs of the project. After making a high-level estimate of the project's size, cost, complexity, risk, and organizational impact, the project team can apply the principles of pragmatic PM to determine just how much project management effort, planning, and documentation are required to support the project.

Applying the five essential elements of pragmatic project management to each project will increase the chance of project success. Sizing each project appropriately, adjusting each essential element of pragmatic PM to scale, and tailoring project management efforts to meet the needs of each unique project will ensure efficiency and effectiveness.

The chapters that follow describe how to scale the five essential elements of pragmatic project management to suit each unique project.

Chapter 2

Pragmatic PM Element #1: The Project Charter

Projects, by their nature, craft something new. They give rise to new products and solutions, enhance existing processes, and change how people work and live their lives. Managing a project is like navigating a boat through open waters: Even if navigation tools abound, the voyage has inherent risk. An experienced sailor will confirm the benefits of pre-planning. In the project management world, preplanning is documented in the project charter. The project charter is the first of the five essential elements of pragmatic project management.

As with sailing through unfamiliar seas, a little planning can help a project manager navigate a project's unknown territory and increase the likelihood of project success. At the very least, project managers must describe the project's main objectives before investing time or money in the effort. Unfortunately, many projects fail because of a lack of clear project direction and planning initially.

THE NEED FOR SPEED VERSUS THE NEED FOR INFORMATION

When a promising new idea excites an organization, it can be difficult to take the time to plan in detail before pursuing the idea. Planning takes time, and everyone wants to get started right away. When time is tight or problems loom large, it is difficult not to just jump into a project or make it up as you go along. Sometimes project particulars seem so obvious that success is simply taken for granted.

Pragmatic PM Rule #3: Projects are always more complex than they seem.

Too often, failing to adequately plan before launching a project ultimately costs the organization a great expense. The truth is that it is difficult to understand exactly how simple or complex an undertaking might be until you take the time to describe it in some detail.

Imagine two hikers looking at the far horizon as they contemplate a short trip across a small valley. The trip is so short that they can see their destination from where they stand. They gaze across the land before them and discuss how they will wind their way down the hillside toward their destination, through the trees, and across a small stream. This couple is in an ideal situation, both as hikers and project managers. Their destination is clear; the trip will be short; they have only two people on their team; and their goal is easy to visualize.

Most projects are more difficult to plan, however, and time always seems tight. Consider the same hikers in a new situation: Now they have a driving need to get out of town and across that valley in a hurry. Even though the couple is somewhat familiar with the route, they have no time to plan. Gathering a few obvious essentials, they get started without checking the weather. A heavy storm develops, and the weather-plagued trek eventually requires more food and equipment than the couple packed.

Pragmatic PM Rule #4: Taking the time to plan prior to undertaking even the smallest project increases the likelihood of success.

Consider the task of planning a convention for thousands of attendees. The budget is sufficient, and time pressures are minimal. A professional event planner sits down with the project sponsor to work through a long list of considerations as she develops the project charter for the project, including:

- Staff requirements
- Pre- and post-event activities
- Public areas, registration areas, and meeting rooms requirements
- Exhibit hall layout and setup
- Business licenses, health and fire permits, and food regulations
- Cleanup and trash removal
- Telecommunications/data transmissions requirements
- Audio, visual, and other technological services.

Addressing each topic takes time, but the experienced event manager understands that the time is well invested when the result is a clear, detailed project charter that communicates the project's objectives and resource requirements.

In one respect, a convention for thousands of people is no different from planning a hike for two. If you understand the project sponsor's vision, have a clear set of objectives, and understand the expected deliverables, you can determine how best to execute the project.

Consider a manager who attends a convention and previews a new piece of software. She returns to her office determined to implement the software, convinced it will make her organization more effective and competitive. Without much consideration or planning, she instructs an IT project team to begin work to implement the software.

The software may in fact have considerable promise, but before long the team and the company are bogged down in a seemingly endless, complex software implementation project. The project has cost much more than the manager initially imagined. The manager and the project team are both frustrated, and soon the project is shut down and declared a failure.

Software development and implementation projects are notoriously complex. Project failure rates in the industry are inordinately high and frequently are the result of spontaneous requirements and technology-driven solutions, rather than well-considered goals, objectives, and planning. In the previous example, a few days of deliberate consideration in advance might have established more realistic expectations and resulted in a comprehensive project charter that supported a good project effort, rather than costly, unproductive knee-jerk excitement over the latest technology.

Realistically, schedule demands may be a factor in any project, particularly when the project addresses an important or urgent business problem. The importance of knowing exactly where you are headed before starting any venture cannot be overstated. Planning upfront will save time and money over the long term.

Too many project stakeholders skip this process, however, even when it could save them substantial time, effort, and resources. That is why the project charter is an essential element of pragmatic project management.

THE PROJECT CHARTER

Taking the time to describe a project before undertaking it can go a long way toward ensuring project success. Consider the project sponsor who said that his agency did not have time to develop project charters; instead of excessive advance planning, he thought that time would be better spent getting the work done. His perception had probably evolved from his own frustration with project managers who spent too much time planning and never got to the work. This perception is often accurate when it involves inexperienced project managers who adopt a specific methodology and stick to it relentlessly without regarding the particular needs of each project. If the project planning effort is not scaled to the specific needs of a project, senseless, costly planning can certainly lead to a waste of time and resources.

Pragmatic PM Rule #5: For every project, aim to conduct only a sufficient amount of advance planning needed to ensure the project's success—no more and no less.

Project managers should aim to conduct only a sufficient amount of advance planning needed to ensure the project's success—no more and no less. A clear, sufficiently detailed project charter provides enough direction needed to orient a project team as it prepares to tackle a project. The project charter, regardless of the nature and scope of the project it describes, includes twelve basic elements:

- Vision – The end state produced by the project, as envisioned by the project sponsor.
- Business problem or opportunity – What the project is launched to address.
- Objectives – The value the project will provide to the organization.
- Deliverables – A description of the end product or service generated by the project.
- High-level schedule – A broad, general outline of key dates impacting the project (e.g., start date, end date, intermediate milestones).
- Constraints – Internal and external factors that could limit the project's scope, schedule, or cost.
- Assumptions – Statements about the project that are believed to be true and could impact the project's scope, schedule, or cost.
- Risks – Potential events that could impact the project's scope, schedule, or cost.
- Team roles and responsibilities – A description of the anticipated project team and its members' skill sets.
- Budget – A high-level estimate of anticipated project costs.
- Scope statement – A description of project parameters; i.e., what will be included in and excluded from the project.
- Sponsor approval – The signature of the project sponsor, authorizing the project and its funding.

Vision

The project vision is a critical element of a good project charter. For a project to be successful, those undertaking it must have a good idea of how to achieve its objectives and whether the goal is worth the effort. Project managers must clearly articulate a vision to the members of the project team and to other project stakeholders.

Pragmatic PM Rule #6: Every project needs a vision: If you can't see it, you can't build it.

A contractor once told clients who wanted to build a new house, "If you can't describe it, I can't build it." When the couple were unable to describe exactly what they wanted, the contractor recommended that they reconsider the project.

In this example, the couple were the project sponsors. By definition, project sponsors authorize and allocate funds to the project. They clearly are in a position to influence the project in meaningful ways. It is the sponsor's vision that launches the investment and charts the course for the project team.

A good project vision statement is brief—usually not more than a paragraph long—and should be clear and easy to explain. To adequately support the project's needs, project stakeholders providing resources must be able to understand the project sponsor's vision. With a clear vision in mind, project stakeholders can stay focused on the right direction and can reorient when obstacles get in their way.

Vision statements laced with technical acronyms and jargon specific to an industry are subject to misinterpretation. Acronyms and jargon common to one industry may not have any meaning to someone working in an entirely different industry. Consider a simple acronym like *PSR*. In the project management world, the initials traditionally stand for *project status report*. In the marketing industry, the acronym might stand for *product sales ratio*. Acronyms and jargon are common and convenient for expediting communications, but they can cause confusion, too.

Business Problem or Opportunity

The business problem or opportunity describes the impetus for the project. The need for a project typically arises from a business problem that requires a solution or an opportunity the business would benefit from facilitating. A basic measure of project success, then, is to consider whether the project solved the problem or facilitated the opportunity.

Objectives

Project objectives identify the specific business value that the project will provide to the organization and provide clear, definitive criteria for project success or failure. Often a number of project objectives spring directly from the project sponsor's vision.

Objectives come in two forms: functional and implied. Functional objectives can be traced directly to the project vision. For example, consider a project vision that includes a new office building constructed within Denver's city limits. The building will provide space for the business's accounting department, which has 100 employees, and it will support a state-of-the-art IT and communications infrastructure.

Several functional objectives can be derived directly from the vision statement:

- This will be a new office, not a renovation.
- The new office will be located within Denver's city limits.
- It will provide office space for 100 accounting employees.
- It will support a state-of-the-art IT and communications infrastructure.

Each of these functional objectives can be traced directly to the vision.

Implied objectives evolve from the more technical aspects of a project. Implied objectives are inherently related to the project's functional objectives and make them achievable. The functional objectives cited above could suggest the following implied objectives:

- Land suitable for the project must be acquired within Denver's city limits.
- The building will meet all Denver and Colorado building code requirements.

All projects have both functional and implied objectives that should provide some value to the organization. It is imperative that all project objectives be traceable to the project vision statement. Any objective that does not support the project vision is extraneous and beyond the scope of the project.

Deliverables

A project ultimately develops a deliverable—a product, service, or other solution—for an organization. While the project vision and objectives are stated in more general terms, the project charter should describe the deliverable in as specific terms as possible and in a clear, succinct manner that can be easily understood and appreciated by all project team members.

High-Level Schedule

Projects, by definition, are time-bound. They are temporary endeavors that exist to generate a deliverable and end once their objectives are fulfilled. As such, there is generally a time frame driving the project and its allocated resources.

Project stakeholders consider and agree upon a high-level schedule in the initial phases of the project, as they develop the project charter. This allows the project sponsor to consider in advance how the project will fit in with existing business operations, budgetary issues, and so on.

Milestones commonly described in the high-level schedule include:

- The project start and end dates
- Go/no-go decision points
- Project planning dates
- Project execution dates
- Customer feedback dates.

The number and nature of the milestones included in the high-level schedule should be modified to meet specific project needs. Simple, small projects may only require a few dates, while a larger, more complex project may need more. The project charter should not include a detailed schedule for the entire project. A detailed schedule is written later, after the project sponsor has approved the project and stakeholders are ready to begin. The project charter frames only the essential elements of the schedule that are needed to formally approve or disapprove a project.

Constraints

Every project has limitations—or constraints—imposed on it by a variety of sources, including budget, schedule, and resource constraints. Constraints are internal and external factors that limit the project's scope, schedule, or cost and help define project boundaries and determine project feasibility.

Documenting constraints will ensure that the project sponsor and the project team appreciate project boundaries. For example, if early estimates suggest that a project will require 12 months to complete, but the project sponsor says that the project must be complete in six months, it may be necessary to reconsider the estimates and the viability of the effort.

Assumptions

Assumptions are statements about the project that are believed to be true and could impact the project's scope, schedule, or cost. The project planning process often involves making assumptions when there is not enough time or information to confirm their veracity.

Assumptions can affect basic understandings of how to deliver the project. If an initial assumption later proves false, all project assumptions and estimates can be thrown into question. For this reason, it is critical to document key project assumptions and to revisit them from time to time, to determine their potential impact on the project and the potential need for re-planning.

Risks

Risks are potential events that could impact the project's scope, schedule, or cost, and they are identified in terms of probability and impact. For example, a project manager might decide a manufacturer has a 50 percent chance of going out of business before it delivers a project's supplies. Another PM might conclude a software developer is only 30 percent likely to successfully code a new software program. These are probability statements.

A risk's impact relates directly to how it could potentially affect project scope, schedule, or cost. The following statements expand upon the two previous examples to incorporate the potential impact the risks could have on the project:

- A manufacturer has a 50 percent chance of going out of business before it delivers a project's supplies. If the manufacturer goes out of business, the project will incur a 25 percent increase in material costs when it shifts to an alternate manufacturer.
- A software developer is only 30 percent likely to successfully code a new software program. If the developer is unsuccessful, the investment made in the developer's time will be lost, and the project will have to restart at an additional cost of $250,000.

If a risk has no potential impact on scope, schedule, or cost, it should not be considered for project planning purposes. For small, simple projects, there is no need to spend a lot of time identifying potential risks. On the other hand, all projects contain some sort of risk, so spending even just a little time considering potential risks is worthwhile.

Team Roles and Responsibilities

The project charter also describes project team roles and responsibilities. As with all forms of business, the predominant portion of a project's costs covers human resources. To successfully estimate a project's potential cost, it is essential to consider the makeup of the project team.

> **Pragmatic PM Rule #7: The predominant portion of a project's costs covers human resources; manage project scope, schedule, and cost estimates accordingly.**

In the early stages of a project, it should be possible to identify all the skill sets required for the project, along with the number of team members needed for each skill set. Good sources of this information are project managers and team members of similar projects or archived project charters from similar projects.

Beyond the estimated number of team members and skill sets required for the project, it is important to identify team roles and responsibilities. This information helps the project sponsor validate the need for each skill set, and it also allows project team members to appreciate the scope of their responsibilities.

Simple tables easily communicate project team roles and responsibilities in a project charter. Figure 2-1 is an extract from an actual list of project team roles and responsibilities used in a project charter.

Figure 2-1 Sample Table Describing Project Team Roles and Responsibilities

Role	Responsibilities
Project Sponsor	• Define strategic vision, assist in project scope management, and convey project importance to internal and external stakeholders ...
Project Advisory Group	• Provide input to the project sponsors on project objectives, priorities, and requirements ...
Project Manager	• Manage the day-to-day tasks of the project ...
...	...

Budget

The project budget is a high-level estimate of anticipated project costs. This estimate is essential for the project sponsor, who makes the go/no-go decision for a potential project. It is also essential for the project manager when preparing to move forward with a new project.

For small projects, the budget estimate may be simple and quite straightforward, without needing additional detail.

Small-project budget: $25,000 for software package, licenses, and labor to configure and install the software

Medium-sized and large projects require more detailed budget estimates to address those projects' increased complexity. Also, the investment in the project is greater; those providing the funding for the project may want more detail about how the project budget will be spent.

Medium-project budget:	$25,000 for software and licenses
	$20,000 for labor to configure the software
	$10,000 for custom software interface with legacy system
	$15,000 for external consultation
	$8,000 for new hardware

Scope Statement

The project scope statement is a description of project parameters; i.e., what will be included in and excluded from the project. It is more than the vision and the statement of objectives, although it includes elements of and should trace to the project's vision and objectives.

To return to the previous example of the office-building project, the scope might include a parking lot for up to 50 employee cars. It might exclude covered parking of any kind, but include at least ten compact slots for visitor parking. The scope might also include the parking lot's direct access to a major arterial road, but exclude any modifications to that road, such as dedicated highway on- and off-ramps.

The project scope provides direction for the development of the project's deliverable, and it may also provide guidance about how the project is to be run. For example, a scope statement may mandate the use of an in-house project manager who is an employee of the sponsoring organization and exclude the use of contract administrative support. It may include a requirement that the project be completed by the end of the coming spring, and it could mandate a budget not to exceed a specific amount.

A well-developed scope statement should be brief and may be in either narrative or outline form. A common approach is to format scope statements as tables listing scope inclusions and exclusions.

It is worth taking the time necessary to clearly delineate the scope of a project, before moving forward with project work. While the other sections of the project charter provide a clear picture of the project's direction and objectives, the scope offers a more focused view of the project's parameters, its deliverables, and its execution.

Sponsor Approval

One purpose behind the project charter is to provide sufficient information for the project sponsor to make a go/no-go decision to authorize the project and its funding. The goal is to describe the project well enough to enable the project sponsor to make a reasoned decision about whether to invest in the effort.

Imagine you are considering whether to join a group on a week-long hiking trip through some place you have never been to before. Intuitively, you feel like the trip might be a good experience, but it will cost a significant amount of money, and you would like more information before you make a commitment. You would likely want to learn more about:

- The destination and its appeal
- When the trip will start and end
- What you will need to take
- Any dangers you might face
- How much it will cost
- The credentials of the organizer.

Knowing this information could help you reasonably decide whether to sign up for the trip or not.

When deciding whether to move forward with a new project, important information to consider includes:

- The project sponsor's vision
- Project objectives
- The business value the project will deliver to the organization
- The project deliverables (e.g., products, services)
- Overall schedule estimates

- Overall resource estimates (e.g., budget, human resources, materials)
- Potential project risks.

An understanding of this information will help you determine whether a project is a wise undertaking.

Once a decision has been made to proceed with a project, the project sponsor should formally approve the project charter and announce the project to the owning organization. Announcing the project validates its importance and is intended to secure the support of other managers in the organization who may be called upon to provide project resources.

SCALING THE PROJECT CHARTER EFFORT

Those who prefer to avoid excessive paperwork and bureaucracy need not balk at the effort required to write a project charter. The charter should simply describe the project and the project team's approach; it does not have to be a lengthy, verbose report. As with all aspects of pragmatic project management, the amount of effort required depends on the characteristics of the project; the goal is to invest minimum effort to achieve maximum gain (Figure 2-2).

There is no minimum page requirement for a project charter. The substance of the document matters, not the number of pages or diagrams. For very small projects, writing a project charter may begin with a simple conversation among project team members over a cup of coffee and scribbles on a napkin. Other times, when more money is at stake and the risks are higher, writing a project charter may require a more deliberate, lengthy process.

The Napkin Approach

Project charters can be long or short. The length of the document and the amount of detail depends on the needs of each project. I once delivered a small IT project using a napkin. My first assignment as a project manager for a consulting company required me to manage an IT project for a small government agency. It was a simple project, with a budget of around

Figure 2-2 Planning Scaling Model

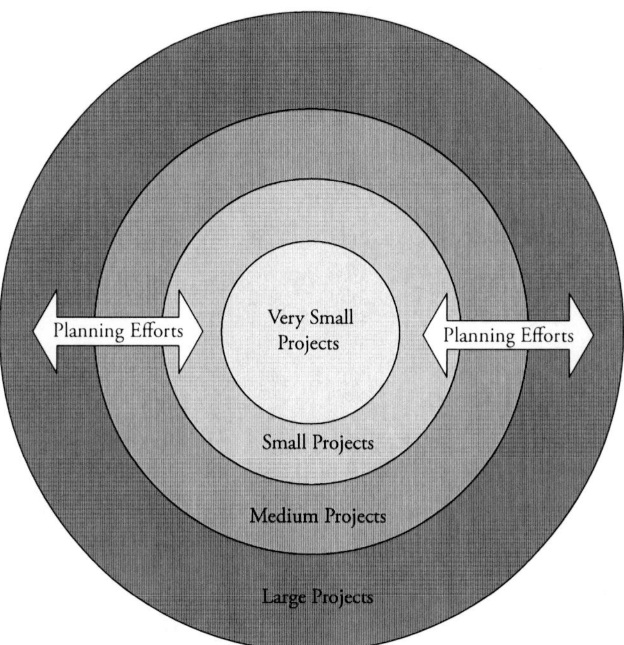

$80,000 and a team consisting of just myself and a technical lead. Our goal was to implement a software package that the agency's manager had learned about watching a demonstration at a professional conference. The project's requirements were clear, and the project sponsor's vision of the deliverable was simple and straightforward.

My project teammate and I discussed the project over a cup of coffee. We estimated it would take six months to flesh out our understanding of the project's principle deliverable: a customized software package. I sketched out the objectives for the project and a few milestones on a napkin lying next to my coffee mug, and we were ready to begin.

The project flew by without a hitch, and the customer was pleased with the results—so pleased, in fact, that it expanded the contract to add more features to the new system. As my supervisor prepared to sign the first contract extension, he asked to see the original project charter. He wanted to use that document as a starting point to meet the expanded contract's new requirements.

When I told him that the project charter included little more than hen scratches on a napkin, he raised an eyebrow. Although we delivered the project successfully—the napkin proved sufficient in this case—he expected us to deliver the next project with a bit more sophistication.

Projects of any size generally require something a bit more substantial than a napkin when it comes to documenting the project charter. Nevertheless, the most important thing was that we had developed a clear project charter before we began work on the project, and the charter had sufficient detail to identify project objectives and our approach.

The Expanded Project Charter

Large and complex projects with challenging objectives require a more substantial investment than small projects, which creates a need for additional information in the project charter. Conscientious project sponsors demand more information before making a decision involving greater investments and risk. An expanded project charter offers more information, even as it answers the same questions as a basic charter: What are the benefits, objectives, risks, and costs to the organization? What approach will the project team take? The difference lies in the level of detail.

For example, a small project might have a simple and direct business problem: The IT vendor no longer supports the current software. This places our business at risk, so we must replace the software.

A larger project might have a more complex set of challenges: The IT vendor no longer supports the current software. The business environment has changed substantially. We must update our capabilities, functionality, and customized user interfaces to support our increasingly sophisticated staff and clients. This places our business at risk, so we must replace the software.

In the two examples, the business-problem statements imply significantly different levels of complexity. The need to expand the basic project charter is driven by such differences in complexity, as well as differences in project risk and the particular needs of the sponsoring organization.

Consider once again the example of the project charter crafted on a napkin for the $80,000 IT project. The customer was so excited by the product that it submitted more than fifty change requests over the next year, increasing the value of the project to more than $1 million. Change requests involved adding functionality and remote technology, which increased associated project risk. Rather than a simple, straightforward software package integration project that affected only one organization, the project expanded to impact two major public agencies, several powerful special-interest groups, and dozens of commercial organizations. Each had a vested interest in the outcome of the project, and as the project grew and investments increased, interest in the project piqued even more.

When the project surpassed $100,000 in value, a document clarifying the customer's expectations was needed, especially to gain buy-in from the numerous stakeholders. We set about transferring the information from the napkin to a more formalized document. The expanded project charter elaborated on the project approach in some detail, formalizing project processes like issue management, change control, budget management, configuration management, test management, and others.

Even then, the project charter was fairly brief, but it clarified the customer's expectations and balanced those expectations with our project plans. Most importantly, the customer's senior representative and sponsor officially signed the charter, explicitly agreeing to the project terms written in the document.

An expanded project charter may start as a basic charter during project initiation and evolve into an expanded document over time. Project managers should never hesitate to re-plan or reshape the project charter as needed.

Beyond the contents of the basic charter, the expanded project charter may include requirements, specifications, stakeholder analysis, criteria for success, details about the planned approach (e.g., the project plan, project initiation activities, project planning activities), and several management plans for categories such as:

- Scope
- Change

- Schedule
- Cost
- Configuration
- Issues
- Resources
- Quality
- Communications
- Requirements
- Risk
- Procurement.

Shape the project charter to meet the needs of the project.

PROJECT CHARTER CHECKLIST

Description	Yes	No	N/A
Vision			
Business problem or opportunity			
Objectives			
Deliverables			
High-level schedule			
Constraints			
Assumptions			
Risks			
Team roles and responsibilities			
Budget			
Scope statement			
Sponsor approval			

EXPANDED PROJECT CHARTER CHECKLIST

Description	Yes	No	N/A
Vision			
Business problem or opportunity			
Objectives			
Deliverables			
High-level schedule			
Constraints			
Assumptions			
Risks			
Team roles and responsibilities			
Budget			
Scope statement			
Sponsor approval			
Requirements			
Specifications			
Stakeholder analysis			
Criteria for success			
Project approach			
Project plan			
Project authorization and initiation activities			
Project planning activities			
Project execution activities			
Project monitoring and control activities			
Project closeout activities			
Additional integrated plans			
Scope management plan			
Change management plan			
Schedule management plan			
Cost management plan			
Configuration management plan			

Description	Yes	No	N/A
Issues management plan			
Resource management plan			
Quality management plan			
Communications management plan			
Requirements management plan			
Risk management plan			
Procurement management plan			

Chapter 3

Pragmatic PM Element #2: The Project Team

Like most business activities, project management primarily involves managing people to reach objectives. Applying appropriate project management tools to plan, execute, monitor, and control a project is important, but only if those tools provide a framework for managing the people fulfilling the project work. When all the planning is done, people execute the project work, and people get the project done. Selecting people and transforming them into a functioning, high-performing project team is a major role of the project manager.

> **Pragmatic PM Rule #8: When all the planning is done, people execute the project work, and people get the project done.**

Only rarely is the PM the sole member of the project team. Most projects have at least two people involved, and often more. However, human resources are expensive, and specific skill sets can be surprisingly scarce. A large team with considerable skills might be desirable, but it will tax a project budget. The project manager must balance the need for specialized project team members with the associated project costs. Pragmatic project management means assembling the minimum number of project team members necessary to deliver the maximum benefit to the project.

Pragmatic PM Rule #9: The right number of project team members is the minimum number necessary to deliver the project effectively.

Assembling the right team can be like going to a restaurant where a new and rare delicacy is on the menu but only in limited supply. You need to place an order early to ensure that what you want is available. In most organizations and industries, experienced, quality experts tend to be in short supply. To ensure those valuable human resources are on your team, make a request for their support early.

Pragmatic PM Rule #10: Identify human resource requirements early.

To assemble the minimum number of project team members necessary to deliver the maximum benefit to the project, employ a combination of full-time, part-time, and contractual project team members just during the part of the project schedule when those members are needed. For example, a project manager might phase project team members into the project schedule according to their role (Figure 3-1):

Figure 3-1 Phasing Project Team Members by Role

Project Team Member	Project Phase
Project Sponsor	Project initiation – Establish the project vision and objectives and authorize the project manager.
Project Manager	Project initiation – Support project charter development.
Technical Lead/Expert	Project initiation – Support project charter development.
Executive Steering Committee	Project initiation – Assist the project sponsor in shaping the project vision and objectives.
Project Advisory Group	Project initiation – Assist in shaping the project sponsor's vision.
Communications Manager	Project initiation – Identify and manage stakeholder expectations.
Change Manager	Project planning and execution – Manage changes to the project and prepare end-users for the deliverable.
Training Manager	Project planning and execution – Identify and plan training requirements.

Project Team Member	Project Phase
Lead Business Analyst	Project planning – Lead requirements analysis efforts.
Business Analyst	Project planning – Support the lead business analyst in project requirements analysis efforts.
Implementation Manager	Project planning and execution – Develop implementation requirements.
Testing Manager	Project planning and execution – Develop test plans, direct incremental testing as required, and finalize plans for end-users.
Subject Matter Experts	Any project phase – Provide subject matter expertise as needed throughout the project.
External Quality Analyst	Project planning – Review project artifacts and processes, and make recommendations for quality improvement.
Independent Verification and Validation Technical Analyst	Project execution – Ensure requirements and specifications trace to project objectives and best practices.
Contractor Team Project Manager	Project planning – After identifying project vision and objectives, incorporate contractor input early in the project.
Contractor Consultant	Any project phase – Provide consulting services as needed throughout the project.
Contractor Senior Business Analyst	Project planning – Support the lead business analyst in project requirements analysis efforts.
Contractor Trainer	Project planning and execution – Identify and plan training requirements.

The project manager does not always have the opportunity to personally shape his or her project team. Sometimes, the project team is already in place when the project manager begins working on a project. If so, the project manager must assess the project and the project team and modify his or her approach to meet the needs of the situation.

Sometimes, joining a project team already in place is particularly difficult, and the PM's frustration about the situation can be distracting. Several years ago, I found myself unexpectedly the president of the local Lions club when the existing club president left the area for a new job. The club's major project each year is Prairie Days, an old-time community fair held over the last weekend in June with a carnival, vendors, entertainment of all kinds, events, and food. It is a big undertaking. The entire city and surrounding countryside turns out for the event; over a dozen police officers direct crowds and traffic.

As president, it became my job to organize and run Prairie Days. As a new member of the club, I knew little about Prairie Days beyond that it happens each year and failure was not an option. Most of the money the club used to help the community throughout the year was raised at the event; no Prairie Days, no club. The pressure was on, and boy, did I feel it.

To make matters worse, two months before the event, the vendor that provided the carnival for the past 20 years retired without notice. Carnival vendors typically schedule their services years in advance; two months was a seemingly impossible hurdle.

I began by inviting the entire club to a meeting to address the situation. At the meeting, club members were quiet and unresponsive. I felt panic rising in my gut, the sort of panic that seasoned project managers can relate to when they see an important project headed south. "This is never going to work," I muttered as I left the clubhouse after the meeting, followed closely by the club secretary. "I can't do all this by myself."

The club secretary, a woman of eighty-plus years and countless Prairie Days events, reached out and smacked me lightly on the back of the head. "You need to delegate, dummy," she said. I turned on my heel and glared at her. "Exactly who am I going to delegate to? They were stone silent in there."

She glared right back at me, although there was the glint of a smile in her eyes. "You read those people wrong during that meeting. They weren't stone silent. They were just waiting for you to ask them to help." She shook her head and chuckled as she turned away and headed for her car. "Some big project manager you are."

I called another meeting a week later and tried a different approach. This time, I made a point of including everyone in the discussion and asked who would be willing to help me plan and run the event. A few minutes later, I had four committees in place, and we were on our way to a successful event.

Pragmatic PM Rule #11: Shape the project approach to complement the project team's character.

Once the committees were in place, each one took ownership of its particular part of the event and assigned individuals to specific tasks. The club committees developed a project plan and executed the plan accordingly. In short order, a new carnival vendor was found, and Prairie Days went off without a hitch, raising more money for the club's charitable account than ever before.

Pragmatic PM Rule #12: Begin delegating work only when a good project team is in place.

The project management axiom that those who do the work should develop the plans makes sense. A project charter developed for a complex IT project is bound to benefit from the collective experience of experts who have participated in similar projects. The Lions club Prairie Days project team members planned the project and executed the plan successfully. The team's involvement in the planning process and its responsibility for making the plans led to the event's ultimate success.

SELECTING A PROJECT TEAM

Project team members have a wide variety of skill sets. From the administrative assistant handling myriad paperwork to the project manager who runs the whole show, a project team can consist of any number of people filling numerous roles.

Exactly how the project team is structured depends on project objectives and the type of work needed to fulfill those objectives. The project charter is the best place to start when determining the constitution of a project team.

For example, if a project is highly technical and the PM lacks the necessary technical skills, he or she must find someone as early as possible with the necessary technical competence. When project costs are high and funding sources are complex and varied (e.g., grants, government appropriations, internal operational budgets, philanthropic donations), the complexities of funding and accompanying reporting requirements may demand an accounting expert as an early member of the project team.

Some projects require a highly formal team structure, and others require a less formal structure. In either case, the project team—be it two people or 20—must fulfill basic roles and responsibilities.

THE FORMAL TEAM

Formally constituted project teams are defined in the project charter and form once the project sponsor approves the charter. Formal teams are commonly associated with organization charts and generally follow a specific professional hierarchy that includes the project sponsor, project manager, and every other person involved in the project (Figure 3-2).

Figure 3-2 Simple Project Organization Chart

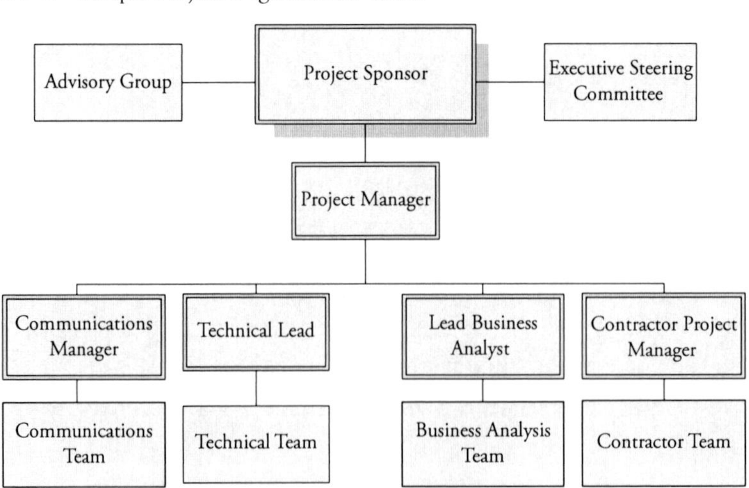

Figure 3-3 presents a list of common project team roles and responsibilities included in an IT project. All the roles in the list could be acquired from the organization's internal resources or, with the exception of the project sponsor, from a contractor. In addition, several roles identified in the list can be fulfilled by a single person working in multiple capacities.

Figure 3-3 Project Team Roles and Responsibilities

Role	Responsibilities
Project Sponsor	• Offer organizational, political, and financial support to the project • Define strategic vision, assist in project scope management, and convey project importance to internal and external stakeholders • Attend executive steering committee (ESC) meetings • Define project vision, goals, and objectives • Resolve high-level issues • Ensure the project supports strategic business objectives • Drive project policy decisions • Communicate with stakeholders, external entities, and partners • Authorize supplemental personnel resources as required • Provide leadership as project champion • Approve changes to project scope, schedule, and budget
Project Manager	• Manage day-to-day project tasks • Attend project meetings • Escalate high-level issues to the project sponsor • Manage the deliverable review process to ensure that deliverables meet organizational goals and objectives • Identify risks and implement risk mitigation strategies • Facilitate and promote stakeholder communication • Maintain project work plans, action-item lists, issue logs, and risk logs • Monitor and report the overall project status • Develop and manage statement of work documentation • Determine project resource requirements, and enlist stakeholder support to obtain these resources • Monitor and track project budget, schedule, and quality against defined project objectives • Ensure contractor compliance
Executive Steering Committee	• Advise the project sponsor on matters pertaining to project scope • Attend regular ESC meetings to address risks and concerns identified by the PM • Determine appropriate changes to organizational policy as recommended by the PM • Set priorities and resolve issues as suggested by the project sponsor

Role	Responsibilities
	• Review issue and risk management activities • Communicate project status and outcomes to internal and external stakeholder groups
Project Advisory Group	• Provide input to the project sponsors on project objectives, priorities, and requirements • Represent the interests and concerns of sponsor organizations and/or constituents (e.g., by addressing issues and risks) • Track issues that may affect stakeholders and their organizations • Provide feedback to ESC and sponsors on project direction • Communicate project progress and results to stakeholders
Technical Lead	• Manage the staff responsible for the functional requirements of the system, system design, and verification activities • Participate in project team activities • Manage day-to-day technical issues • Support the development staff's technical requirements • Coordinate activities with end-users to assist in resolving interface issues
Communications Manager	• Oversee all internal and external communications activities • Develop and maintain the communications plan and documentation • Support the development of project status reports • Develop stakeholder communications plans • Implement communications plan tasks and activities • Oversee the management of the project library
Change Manager	• Facilitate appropriate changes to organizational procedures, operations, and systems • Ensure project activities are integrated and coordinated with other organizational initiatives and projects • Prepare staff for project implementation
Training Manager	• Manage all training activities and deliverables (e.g., the training plan, curriculum, and schedule; train-the-trainer activities) • Provide oversight for training activities • Review and approve IT vendor-supplied training materials and documentation • Ensure that end-users receive appropriate and timely training suited to their needs • Participate in project team meetings
Business Analyst Lead	• Ensure that the project supports stated user requirements • Identify project interface requirements with other projects and operations within and outside the organization • Develop design documentation for any customizations

Role	Responsibilities
	• Support and coordinate the release management cycle • Manage the business analyst staff assigned to the project • Interpret business requirements for technical staff during design, development, and test activities • Participate in project team meetings
Business Analyst	• Work with end-users to define functionality requirements • Define business process flows impacting and driving the project • Design analytical views, key performance indicators, and dashboard requirements • Participate in project team meetings
Implementation Manager	• Develop and execute implementation plans • Coordinate agency and contractor project teams' activities in accordance with duties defined by the project manager • Communicate project status information to the project team • Manage pilot and production rollout activities focusing on field implementation • Prepare implementation team resources for implementation activities • Perform technical-readiness activities • Prepare help desk personnel to support the deliverable once implemented • Participate in project team meetings
Testing Manager	• Coordinate test development and execution activities • Organize people, facilities, and equipment needed for testing • Coordinate IT vendor preparation for testing/accepting the deliverable • Ensure traceability between the solution delivered by the IT vendor and approved project requirements • Ensure the IT vendor maintains requirements documentation to support traceability • Review IT vendor deliverables and reports for acceptance and defects • Manage the resolution of testing issues • Track defects until resolved • Participate in project team meetings
Subject Matter Experts	• Represent end-user and business needs • Facilitate the resolution of business and technical issues • Support testing activities • Support training activities • Review deliverables, and provide feedback to ensure the deliverables meet business needs • Support the definition of interface requirements and testing • Participate as a "super-user" during implementation planning and when coordinating for end-users • Assist in identifying, tracking, and resolving project issues, risks, changes, and problems

Role	Responsibilities
	• Assist in defining requirements • Serve as an advocate of change as appropriate
External Quality Assurance Analyst	• Review project activities and project management processes • Review project deliverables • Provide project sponsors with an independent assessment of project processes and products to ensure that the project meets the objectives identified by the sponsor • Regularly report assessments to project sponsors, including project risks and recommended mitigation strategies • Investigate or provide an independent assessment of project issues as needed, and make recommendations to address issues • Identify concerns related to project performance and success • Ensure that the project follows industry and organizational standards
Independent Verification and Validation (IV&V) Technical Analyst	• Confirm initial project definition • Develop the IV&V approach and plan throughout the project • Provide routine IV&V reports to the project sponsor and ESC • Offer recommendations for course corrections • Keep a log of findings and recommendations • Meet regularly with the PM • Review deliverables

For many projects, it is common for organizations to hire contractors with specific skill sets. In those instances, additional contractor roles and responsibilities should be considered for the project team (Figure 3-4):

Figure 3-4 Project Contractor Roles and Responsibilities

Role	Responsibilities
Contractor Team Project Manager	• Provide project leadership • Control contractor project activities, providing leadership and direction • Establish and oversee project management controls for issue, change, and risk management • Develop project plans and manage contractor project resources • Work cooperatively with agency team members to develop deliverables • Participate in project team and ESC meetings
Senior Consultant	• Apply specific expertise to the project, as required by the project contract and the needs of the contractor project manager • Participate in project team activities as required

Role	Responsibilities
Consultant	• Work with subject matter experts (SMEs) to validate as-is business processes • Work with SMEs to design to-be business processes • Work with the training manager to help develop training materials • Work with the testing manager to structure and manage testing efforts • Facilitate issue resolution
Developer	• Develop and configure business solutions that comply with approved user requirements and all other contract deliverables • Respond to product defects, errors, and user concerns until resolved
Trainer	• Direct and oversee contractor staff responsible for developing training strategies, programs, and support materials • Organize and coordinate contractor-supplied training • Schedule and manage training delivery for agency staff and end-users

Given all the potential roles, responsibilities, and skill sets, how do you choose a project team, and how do you decide when specific team members should begin working during project execution? As a general rule, most projects require at least three project team members, including:

- Project sponsor – Authorizes and funds the project
- Project manager – Leads and manages day-to-day project operations
- Technical lead – Applies the sophisticated technical expertise needed to address project objectives and requirements.

The rationale behind the project sponsor's early involvement is obvious: The sponsor authorizes and funds the project. A project cannot move forward without the sponsor's approval. Later, when the project requires a decisionmaker with more authority than the PM, the project sponsor must make those decisions to ensure that the project progresses.

The PM leads and manages the project, forms the project team, and facilitates project planning, execution, and closeout. A project manager is essential from the very first days of the project.

The technical lead understands the complex aspects of the project and provides the skills and experience necessary to construct a building, design a software system, lay out a major carnival, or orchestrate food service for a convention. The technical lead's skills and experience help provide the team with a comprehensive understanding of project complexities.

Occasionally, the technical lead and the project manager are the same person, although this can be problematic. The technical lead is at times buried in intense deliberation over technical issues, and it can be very difficult to separate the technical aspects of the project and the need for basic PM leadership and oversight.

Other members of the project team are brought on board as project requirements dictate. In formal project structures, each new member of the team works directly or indirectly for the project manager. The project manager should always report directly to the project sponsor.

The project sponsor often plays an on-again, off-again role in the project, called in to make decisions extending beyond the basic team's authority. Most of the leadership and decision-making work, however, is left to the project manager and the technical lead.

THE INFORMAL TEAM

For very small projects, the project team may consist of no more than two or three people coming together over a cup of coffee to discuss a simple business need. Their loose coalition of skill sets and personalities may be all that is required to successfully deliver a solution to the business need.

When any number of people cooperate to tackle any type of task, roles evolve out of the need to get things done. These roles are dictated by the situation, the experience and comfort levels of participants, and the specific needs of the project. Members of informal coalitions often fulfill each of the basic skill sets normally involved in any project, regardless of the project's size. One person typically steps forward as the team's leader, acting as a project manager. Another team member might address technical aspects of the project, and a third might be responsible for finding funds and other resources needed to get the job done. Often the members of small teams will share many roles and responsibilities.

PROJECT, FUNCTIONAL, MATRIX, AND HYBRID TEAMS

The structure of the project team ultimately depends on a variety of factors, such as the culture of the organization, project management experience, and available funds and human resources. Project teams generally evolve out of one of four types of organizations:

- Project organization
- Functional organization
- Matrix organization
- Hybrid organization.

Project Organization Project Teams

In a project organization, human resources assigned to the team work directly for the project manager, who has full responsibility for supervising and evaluating team members and plays a direct role in each team member's professional life. The project organization structure gives the project manager direct control over team members (Figure 3-5).

Figure 3-5 Example Project Organization Project Team Structure

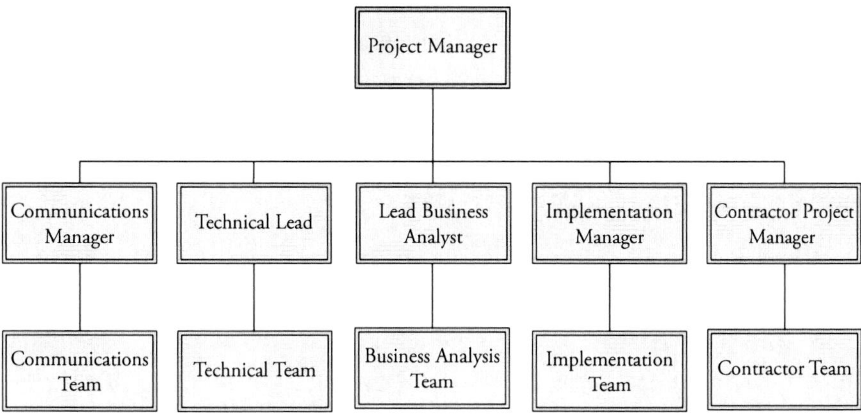

In one of my first assignments as a project manager, I worked for a major company that created flight simulators. The company was organized into two major divisions: project management and production. As a PM, I worked on a specific flight simulator project in an office with all the

other project team members. A program manager responsible for multiple flight simulator projects oversaw, managed, and evaluated my performance.

The project team worked closely together and built a tight-knit, family-like culture that resulted in many close professional and personal relationships. We had a strong sense of accountability, and when the company delivered a flight simulator to customers, every team member shared in the success. Much of the company's reputation stemmed from the commitment of each team member—a commitment fostered by the company's project organization structure.

The project organization structure does not in and of itself create a perfect project team. The project manager must still lead, manage, train, and mentor his or her team to inspire everyone to give their best effort.

Functional Organization Project Teams

In functional organizations, the project manager may be the only person directly assigned to the project and whose primary role is to work on that particular project. All the other project team members typically report to functional managers in other areas of the organization. Those team members are essentially on loan to the project to complete particular tasks, but they also continue working in their primary jobs when the project manager doesn't need their assistance. Functional team members are not evaluated by the project manager in terms of advancement or promotion within the organization. As a result, the project manager has no direct authority over the team members (Figure 3-6).

In the functional organization project team structure, the project's accounting specialist continues to work for the accounting department. The technical lead or project engineer continues to work for the engineering department. Business experts and analysts continue to work for the business development team, and so on.

To support project objectives, the PM must build relationships, negotiate, and communicate with the functional managers who provide the human resources making up the project team. If the PM has good working relationships with functional managers, the project can go very well;

Figure 3-6 Example Functional Organization Project Team Structure

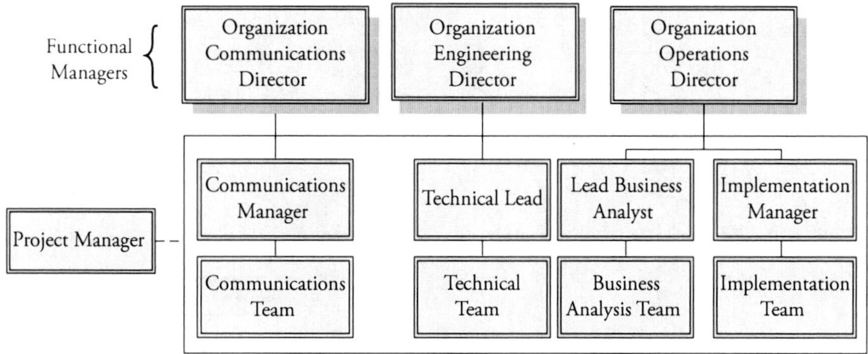

if not, difficulties can arise. When project managers and functional managers compete for human resources, the PM often takes second seat.

Relationships between project managers and functional managers must be supported by the commitment of the project sponsor. If the project sponsor is a senior executive who directly oversees functional managers, the PM can escalate project issues to the sponsor for help resolving those issues. The sponsor is ultimately responsible for directing the project to align with greater organizational business objectives.

Matrix Organization Project Teams

In the matrix organization, the functional manager and project manager share joint supervisory responsibility over project team members. Both have input into project team members' performance evaluations and opportunities for advancement within the organization and on the project team (Figure 3-7).

As in functional project organizations, the success of matrix organizations' projects is greatly impacted by relationships between functional managers and project managers. However, in matrix organizations, project managers have greater control, which allows project team members to more easily affirm their membership and commitment to the project team.

Figure 3-7 Example Matrix Organization Project Team Structure

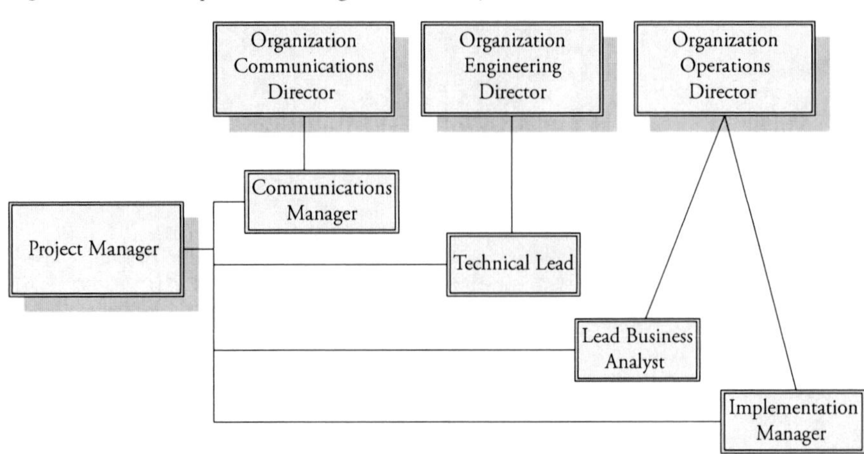

Matrix organizations are common in highly projectized industries, such as engineering, construction, and software industries, where individuals are required to support multiple projects simultaneously. Consider the design engineer required to create specifications for a new aircraft: His or her involvement in a new aircraft design effort would be intense during the early phases of planning and periodically during manufacturing and testing. When the design engineer is not preoccupied by that project, however, he or she could be working on other projects, which is a more effective way to utilize this highly valuable and often expensive resource.

In matrix organizations it is common for resources like the design engineer to be primarily assigned to a particular department that provides specific technical support, professional guidance, and education. The design engineer would then also fulfill periodic assignments on specific projects and report both to the director of his or her department and to the project manager; both the department director and the project manager would share responsibility for the performance evaluation of that individual.

Hybrid Organization Project Teams

Rigid organizational models do not always provide the best structure for every project. Sometimes combining organizational models to form a hybrid project team structure facilitates the particular needs of an organization (Figure 3-8).

Figure 3-8 Example Hybrid Organization Project Team Structure

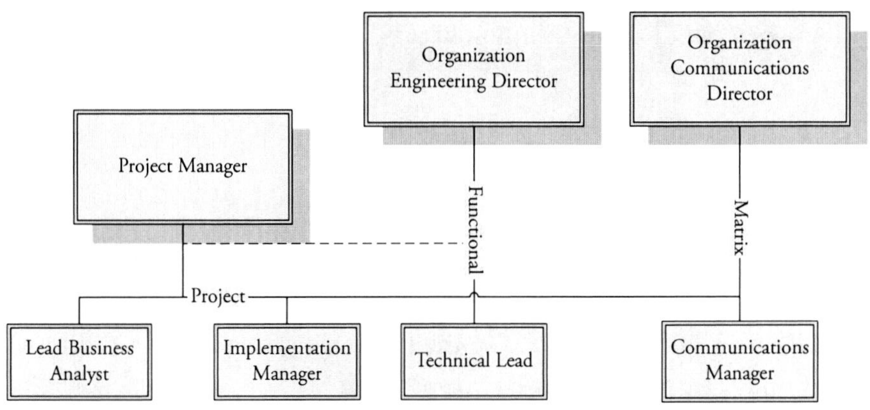

My experience at the flight simulator company provides an example of how hybrid project organizations evolve. As I described previously, that company was a project organization. My first boss was an integrated logistics manager who worked for a project manager in charge of specific flight simulator projects. That project manager reported to a program manager who managed a number of flight simulator projects.

This organizational model worked well for several years until the company was issued several large contracts and resources became scarce. When that happened, one individual was often needed for multiple projects, so a matrix organizational structure evolved. An individual from the engineering drawing team, for example, was assigned to a project temporarily while he still reported to his functional manager. This is typical in functional organizations. Other project members remained assigned exclusively to a single project, maintaining the original project organization team structure. Together, the company formed a hybrid organization to address its particular needs.

Organizations should not hesitate to improvise and develop hybrid project team structures as needed. As long as project teams are responsive, lean, and agile, and as long as the team structure yields a productive, positive working environment, the project has a good chance at success.

Pragmatic PM Rule #13: Organizations should not hesitate to improvise and develop hybrid project team structures as needed.

STAKEHOLDERS

A stakeholder is anyone with a vested interest in the outcome of a project. The number of stakeholders can become too high for those individuals to reasonably be considered a part of the project team, per se. Instead, stakeholders work on the periphery of the project team, providing occasional input and ideas and helping to keep the project on track. They confer directly with the project sponsor and may be members of the project advisory committee or executive steering committee.

Stakeholder management is a communications issue. Stakeholders can be invited as active participants in the project, or they can be ignored. Powerful stakeholders typically do not remain quiet for very long when ignored. If stakeholders feel underappreciated, they can use their political, professional, or personal clout to impose their will on the project. These situations most often manifest as surprise scope changes the team must address at considerable expense or as additional meetings and reports where project leadership is called to explain why stakeholders have been overlooked and why their input has not been solicited.

Instead, project managers should involve stakeholders in the project as much as possible when appropriate. Project managers should identify and manage stakeholders, soliciting their input early and often throughout the project lifecycle. Stakeholders offer critical project information. Incorporating this information minimizes impact to the project's schedule and cost over time. The amount of effort PMs should expend on stakeholder management depends on each stakeholder's potential impact to the project and on the nature of its stake in the project—i.e., how it is invested in the project deliverables.

Pragmatic PM Rule #14: Manage stakeholders attentively to avoid costly problems later.

CRITICAL TEAM MANAGEMENT FACTORS

Managing people as part of teams or as stakeholders can be challenging. No matter the project size or complexity, project teams and stakeholders require some leadership. The PM is responsible for critical team management factors like leadership and team building.

Leadership

Getting a team of athletes ready to compete in a sporting event is a project: Each event is temporary, requires planning and preparation, and has a defined goal—victory. Coaches are project managers: They unite the team and plan the team's development, taking a group of individual athletes with varying degrees of talent and turning them into a cohesive, competitive force.

History is full of coaches whose strong leadership skills took teams with sub-par talent to the highest levels of achievement, often against long odds. Conversely, history is also full of coaches who led teams of highly talented athletes without bringing them together to achieve victory.

A great project manager with leadership skills inspires a project team to surpass its limitations to achieve success. These leaders have vision and communicate that vision clearly and passionately. Great project managers lead by example, inspiring their teams to high levels of performance even in difficult situations and keeping the team focused under pressure. These leaders know how to celebrate success and reward their team when it accomplishes a significant goal.

Leadership skills can be developed through experience and training. Project managers who focus on applying sound leadership principles to each project will solidify the skills needed to lead any team to project success.

Team Building

Teams evolve through several distinct stages once they come together for any purpose, passing through phases of function and dysfunction before developing into an effective team. Without leadership, teams may actually self-destruct and disband. Some project teams get bogged down as they wrestle with competing political influences and interests and disagree about project objectives and requirements.

Teams require PM leadership to become high-performing units. Project managers can facilitate team-building exercises to solidify the group into one that can successfully fulfill project objectives on time and under budget. Myriad team-building exercises are available to help project managers bring a team together; PMs can find team-building resources online or through books, consultants, and training companies specializing in leadership and team development.

No matter how a project manager approaches team building, it is imperative that he or she recognizes the need and takes decisive action to bring the project team together. PMs must take a proactive approach to team building. With tight project schedules and scanty budgets common throughout the industry, project managers cannot afford to waste time and funds waiting for a project team to become a cohesive unit on its own.

SCALING PROJECT TEAM MANAGEMENT

No matter the size or complexity of the project, project teams should be kept as small as possible, with the right balance of skill sets needed to deliver the final product or service. The potential for communications problems increases proportionally with the team's size. The more people involved in the communications chain, the more often messages can be misinterpreted, reinterpreted, or garbled. For example, a project team made up of just six members yields fifteen lines of communication (Figure 3-9).

A simple equation where *n* is the number of people yields the number of lines of communication:

$$\frac{n(n-1)}{2}$$

Using this equation, one can calculate the lines of communication among 20 people, for example:

$$\frac{20(20-1)}{2} = 190$$

Figure 3-9 Lines of Communication among Six People

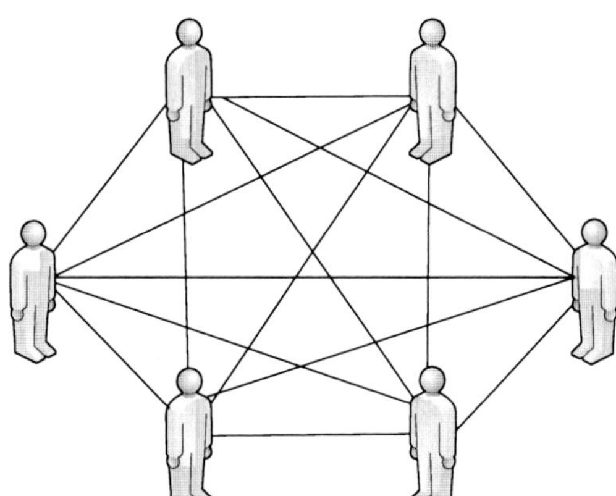

A team of 20 members has 190 lines of communication, which must all be managed by the project manager.

The project manager of a team with three members can afford to manage communications informally. With only three lines of communication, it is relatively easy to keep communications clear and organized. No matter how small the project, however, team members should always meet periodically to ensure that everyone understands project details.

Consider three people working together to develop a new company policy that will impact a labor agreement in an organization. On such a small team, ensuring that all team members are working in concert would seem fairly simple. If one member of that team takes a vacation for two weeks, however, and returns to find that the other two team members have left the project suddenly for various reasons, the situation gets complicated.

The other two team members left without communicating important stakeholder change requests. When newspaper reporters arrive to inquire about the new policy and its potential impact on important labor agreements, the remaining team member presents only the facts he knows, without an awareness of the change requests received while he was away. The reporters depart and publish their articles in good faith.

Immediately stakeholders want to know why their change requests weren't acknowledged in the press.

Even small teams require management. This three-person team would have benefited from a simple notes file documenting the latest project developments and issues. That way, the team member returning from vacation could read through the notes file to quickly learn the latest project status. Without this basic tool, he was lost.

A roles and responsibilities chart is another basic tool good for use on project teams of any size. (A sample is provided in Figure 3-3.) The roles and responsibilities chart serves as a point of reference for the project manager, who needs to determine who could best handle a specific issue or task, and for the project team member, who needs guidance to help focus his or her efforts. A roles and responsibilities chart can also help team members refer tasks, questions, or issues to other, more appropriate project team members as necessary.

The project manager should take the size of a project team into consideration when deciding whether to formalize team communications, roles, and responsibilities. Some may balk at the prospect of developing yet another plan or matrix for a project, but often that very plan or matrix provides just the right touch of formality to avoid the challenges associated with complex communications networks.

SCALING THE PROJECT TEAM

As with all aspects of pragmatic project management, the goal is to expend minimum effort to achieve maximum project gain. Small projects should employ small project teams. This minimizes the communications requirements and ensures a tighter, more focused group. Larger projects should employ larger project teams to distribute project work efficiently. The core project team should remain minimal, expanding to include additional resources only as necessary. The goal is to scale the project team—and therefore, the effort it takes to manage the team—to meet only the particular needs of the project (Figure 3-10).

Figure 3-10 Project Team Scaling Model

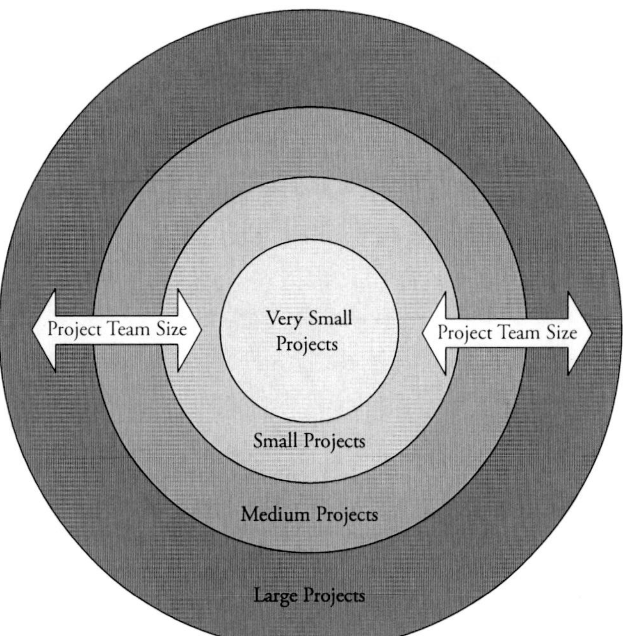

The project sponsor and the project manager must scale the project team's size to meet specific project needs. When the project charter is developed early in the project lifecycle, it can be difficult to accurately estimate the right size of a project team. The need for additional skill sets and team members is commonly discovered as the project moves into latter phases of planning and execution. Project leadership must acknowledge this possibility and plan accordingly.

In the late 1990s, I managed a project commissioned to renovate parts of an old hospital, to bring the building up to code and to facilitate patient needs. The approved scope of the project included re-plumbing the west wing, which housed half of the hospital's patient beds, and replacing all the hospital's exterior windows. The estimated project cost totaled just over $6.9 million.

Contractors would complete much of the project work. We initially decided that necessary hospital resources would include a project manager, an engineering technician conversant with plumbing, and a contracts specialist. As needed, we would ask nursing personnel from the patient wards and other areas to assist in relocating the patients during peak project periods.

A few weeks into the project, a plumber encountered what appeared to be asbestos. We immediately called in our facilities manager, who had experience with asbestos abatement. He suggested that we hire an asbestos abatement specialist to consult and assist us in hiring a contractor to remove the asbestos. Following that suggestion, we added both the asbestos consultant and facilities manager to the project team.

Later, a plumber identified old, faulty wiring while tracing the pipes through hospital walls. We once again called our facilities manager, who suggested we expand the project scope to inspect and replace any problem wiring encountered while re-plumbing. We complied, and our project team increased in size again with the addition of a full-time electrician and part-time electrical engineer.

In a period of just three weeks, our project team more than doubled. The only aspect of the project that remained unchanged throughout the ten months of the project lifecycle was the window replacement, which went off without a hitch.

This example is not uncommon. Projects inherently include a degree of risk and unpredictability. Project change is inevitable, but if change is appropriately managed, the project sponsor and project manager can assess project resource needs and re-plan as necessary.

Pragmatic PM Rule #15: Never be afraid to re-plan, particularly where team membership is involved.

Scaling a project's team requirements is a four-step process:

1. Identify the skill sets needed for the project.
2. Define the work required for each skill set (e.g., design development, requirements analysis, artifact development).

3. Convert the work into time packages that can be assigned to resources.
4. Schedule resources to align with the work required at each stage of the process.

Using data from analogous projects can expedite this process.

Identify Required Skill Sets

Developing the project charter during the initial phases of the project includes forming a rough, high-level estimate of the work required for each skill set. For example, a project sponsor, project manager, and technical or business lead are typically required for any team. Projects with unique complexities may require other roles and responsibilities. A high-level estimate is sufficient to complete the project charter; lacking more detailed information at this stage should not delay the project.

Define the Work

As the PM develops the project schedule or expands the project charter to include more detail, additional information—e.g., design specifications, a risk management plan, a change management plan, business or technical architecture, a quality assurance plan—may reveal a need for additional skill sets.

Convert Work into Time Packages

The PM estimates the duration of specific work requirements and identifies those estimates as time packages. He or she then identifies the relationship between each time package—e.g., time package A must occur before time package B, or the two can happen at the same time—and orders all the packages to ensure the project progresses appropriately.

Schedule Appropriate Resources

After more fully identifying the skills needed for the work, the PM can align the appropriate resources with project timelines. In this manner, the

PM can build a project team according to the specific skills needed to deliver the product or service, and he or she can schedule resources during only the periods they are needed, keeping the team lean throughout the project lifecycle.

Use Data from Analogous Projects

When embarking on a project that shares specific similarities with past analogous projects, PMs can use that historical information to build a new project team—e.g., which skills sets were employed, how resources were phased into the project schedule. Of course, it is important to assess whether the analogous project team was successful, and adjustments on current, unique projects are always required, but taking advantage of relevant historical project information can support any team-development effort.

PROJECT TEAM PLANNING CHECKLIST

Description	Y	N	N/A
Develop a project plan to identify work requirements.			
Identify skill sets needed to support work requirements.			
Convert work into time packages.			
Estimate project team costs against project team requirements, and review the project plan and skill set requirements with the project sponsor. Secure project sponsor approval to proceed with the project.			
Recruit and schedule resources to align with the work required at each stage of the process.			
Orient and train new team members as they begin work on the project.			
Manage and control resources according to the project plan.			

Chapter 4

Pragmatic PM Element #3: The Project Plan

The average traveler has some idea about his or her destination. With a firm destination in mind, the traveler can plan carefully, increasing his or her chance of a successful trip. Some travelers appreciate complete spontaneity, but that generally requires an indifference to time and money. The project manager, however, is never indifferent to time and money, and when resources are constrained, having a clear knowledge of project objectives and how to achieve them is paramount. Wasted time means additional cost. Having a plan for completing the project improves the likelihood of overall success.

Pragmatic PM Rule #16: Every project needs a plan.

The project plan lays out each major project task scheduled for all phases of the project lifecycle. Each element of the project plan supports the project sponsor's vision of the project deliverable. Specifically stated or implied within the project sponsor's vision are objectives that clarify the business value provided by the project deliverable. Project requirements are the individual components or functionality of the deliverable needed to fulfill project objectives. Any element of the project plan that cannot trace from a requirement to an objective is out of scope.

Whenever possible, the project team members who will do the work should develop the corresponding portion of the plan, with guidance and direction from the project manager. Once approved by the project sponsor, the project plan is the official baseline approach to the project. Any changes to the plan must be approved by the project manager and project sponsor in accordance with the project scope management plan.

Pragmatic PM Rule #17: Whenever possible, the project team members who will do the work should develop the corresponding portion of the project plan, with guidance and direction from the project manager.

THE VISION STATEMENT

Some projects begin with a crystal-clear vision statement issued by the project sponsor; other projects begin with much less. A vision statement for an IT project might specify a new automated financial accounting system with integrated accounts receivable, accounts payable, inventory management, grants management, and general ledger. For a construction project, the vision statement might include offices for the accounting department with state-of-the-art equipment and communications devices, full accessibility for disabled workers, and basement space for the company's biological research and development facility.

Projects without a clear vision statement start with a significant impediment. The project sponsor might have a vague idea that the organization needs a new accounting system, but lack an understanding of exactly what the new system should entail. Perhaps the existing grant management system is adequate, but the general ledger requires new software. Some commercial off-the-shelf software packages might suffice without exactly meeting the business need or offering as much functionality as a custom-built financial management system. The absence of perfect information can misdirect a project.

The clarity of the project sponsor's vision dictates the likelihood of project success. The project manager should ensure that the project sponsor provides a clear vision statement as early as possible during the project. The project sponsor may not recognize the impact a vision statement has on project success. The PM must convey this importance and ensure that the project team benefits from a clear vision statement.

Pragmatic PM Rule #18: The clarity of the project sponsor's vision dictates the likelihood of project success.

PROJECT OBJECTIVES

Project objectives relay the business value intended by fulfilling the project. The objectives are an extension of the vision statement's major components—and should always trace back to that statement—and they identify the value that project deliverables will offer to the end-user.

Pragmatic PM Rule #19: Objectives should always trace directly to the vision statement issued by the project sponsor.

While the vision statement provides the general direction for the project, the objectives provide specific guidance that keeps the project on course from beginning to end, with checkpoints along the way. Identifying clear project objectives guides the project manager and project team as they determine the best path to satisfy the project sponsor's vision. Without objectives, the project manager and team members can easily get off track, wasting valuable time and risking excessive scope creep and project failure.

Pragmatic PM Rule #20: Clear project objectives provide essential guidance throughout the project.

Consider the vision statement for a construction project that specifies a new office building with sufficient parking for company staff and visitors. Elaborating on that vision, the following objectives might emerge:

The new parking lot shall provide parking for the company's 60 staff members and approximately 40 daily visitors. The lot shall also provide space for the temporary parking of delivery vehicles. The farthest parking space shall be within 500 yards of the building's main entrance. The lot shall provide accessible parking in accordance with Americans with Disabilities Act (ADA) guidelines; accommodate compact cars and van-pool vehicles; provide emergency-vehicle access; and include a covered waiting area for a single metro transit drop-off site. Lot construction shall be funded by the greater office-building construction project budget. The lot shall be constructed in the space identified for parking in the approved plat drawings, and it shall be completed prior to opening the new office building.

Objectives spring directly from the project sponsor's vision statement. They elaborate on that vision by providing more specificity, but without extending beyond the project sponsor's intentions. If, for example, the project sponsor envisions a building with adequate parking for 60 company employees, the project's scope should not expand to include a paid parking garage for several hundred cars, even if that would provide an opportunity to raise revenue for the organization.

Some objectives are directly implied by the project sponsor's vision. These objectives are generally technical in nature. One of the objectives cited previously, for example, is ADA compliance. This translates into a more technical, specific objective that a specific percentage of total parking spaces must be handicap-accessible.

One way to determine whether an objective is appropriate for the project is to assess whether it is a S.M.A.R.T. objective. *S.M.A.R.T.* is an acronym meaning *specific*, *measurable*, *achievable*, *realistic*, and *time-bound*:

- Specific – Objectives identify deliverables and are not generalities.
- Measurable – Objectives are measurable, i.e., quantifiable.
- Achievable – Objectives are attainable within existing project constraints and limitations.
- Realistic – Objectives are not pipe dreams or pies in the sky.
- Time-bound – Objectives are attainable within a specific time frame.

The following S.M.A.R.T. assessment of the parking lot objectives previously outlined shows that the objectives are thorough and appropriate:

- Specific – The lot shall provide parking spaces for staff, visitors, delivery vehicles, disabled employees, and designated vehicle types, and it shall also provide access to metro transit customers.
- Measurable – The lot shall accommodate 60 staff members and approximately 40 daily visitors. The farthest parking space shall be within 500 yards from the building's main entrance. Twenty percent of the parking spaces shall be handicap-accessible.
- Achievable – If adequate space and resources are available and the cost is within the project's budget, the objective is achievable.
- Realistic – Providing there are no unforeseen impediments regarding land, budget, resources, etc., the project is realistic.
- Time-bound – The parking lot shall be finished before the office building opens.

Pragmatic PM Rule #21: Good project objectives are always S.M.A.R.T.—specific, measurable, achievable, realistic, and time-bound.

REQUIREMENTS

With objectives firmly established, the next step in building a good project plan is to identify deliverable requirements—specific attributes that satisfy project objectives. Requirements should trace directly to objectives, just as objectives should trace directly to the project vision statement. As a rule, requirements that do not trace to any objectives are out of scope. One way to ensure traceability is to document each requirement-objective relationship in writing.

Pragmatic PM Rule #22: Requirements should trace directly to project objectives; requirements that do not trace to any objectives are out of scope.

Imagine once again a hiker planning a trek and considering what is needed to reach his or her final destination. One requirement is to find a good trail head or starting point where the hiker can park before embarking on the journey. Other requirements might include essential supplies like canteens and drinking water. Without fulfilling such requirements, the hiker's journey would be much more difficult. Experienced hikers understand the importance of identifying what is necessary before heading into the wilderness.

Small projects are like short hikes in that they might not include a lot of requirements. Larger projects, like multi-day hikes across more difficult terrain, might include more complex, numerous requirements. Compare the requirements for constructing a paper airplane versus those for constructing a large, jet-powered airplane. The paper airplane requires a piece of paper and a few folds. The jet-powered aircraft has thousands of requirements, including complexities like fuselage and fly-by-wire avionics.

Specified Requirements

The parking lot objectives states several requirements outright:

- The parking lot shall include parking spaces for 60 staff.
- The parking lot shall include parking spaces for 40 daily visitors.
- The parking lot shall include temporary parking space for delivery vehicles.
- The parking lot shall extend no more than 500 yards from the building's main entrance.
- The parking lot shall be in compliance with ADA standards for handicap-accessible parking.
- The parking lot shall include parking spaces that accommodate economy cars and van-pool vehicles.
- The parking lot shall include emergency-vehicle access space.
- The parking lot shall include a metro transit drop-off area.
- The parking lot construction project shall use the office-building construction budget.
- The parking lot shall utilize available space within approved plat drawings.
- The parking lot shall be completed project prior to opening the new office building.

The objectives' wording made it easy to identify specified requirements. Additional or implied requirements must also be considered.

Implied Requirements

Implied requirements are generally technical in nature and typically require the assistance of a subject matter expert to identify. While specified requirements spring directly from project business objectives, implied requirements identify attributes that are not apparent in the wording of the business objective but are just as necessary as specified requirements.

In an IT project, for example, a business objective might be to provide an accounts payable module for a financial accounting system. An implied requirement might indicate the need for a specific type of server or network architecture. Implied requirements of the parking lot objectives might include the following:

- The parking lot shall include one handicap-accessible parking space for every 25 regular parking spaces.
- The parking lot shall have zero transition access from accessible parking spaces to public walkways; i.e., no curbs, vertical dividers, or enclosed areas shall impede the progress of disabled persons during their movement through, to, and from the parking lot to the building entrance.
- The design engineer shall provide evidence of an approved environmental-impact statement.
- The parking lot shall include a rainwater capture and drainage pond.
- The parking lot shall have an asphalt surface underlain by a specific type of aggregate, depending on the nature of the site's geologic substructure.
- Each parking space shall be marked according to the county's building code.
- The parking lot shall include a pedestrian crosswalk with a traffic warning light.
- The parking lot shall include an arterial turn lane.

Building a project plan involves dissecting project objectives to identify specified and implied requirements, providing a clear view of project deliverables and framing the project's scope.

Pragmatic PM Rule #23: Specified and implied requirements frame the project's scope.

To identify the work needed to satisfy specific project requirements, the PM can reference the following:

- Data from analogous, successful projects
- Team member past experience
- Commercial sources (e.g., project task lists and estimates purchased from industry experts or developed using project simulation software).

PROJECT TASKS

Project tasks are the work needed to satisfy the project's requirements and provide a specific course for the project to follow from beginning to end. When all the project tasks are accumulated and organized logically, they form the project plan.

One requirement might result in many tasks. For example, if a project is launched to construct a new software system, and one requirement is to develop a data-sharing capability between the new system and an existing software system, then the development of an interface between those two systems is a derivative requirement, too.

The work needed to develop that interface can be simple and straightforward or complex and challenging, depending on the specific business need and the technology available to develop the system. If the interface requires only a flat file pushed from one system to another, generating that interface will be a relatively simple process. If the interface requires an XML schema and active data transfer between the systems in real time, then generating that interface may be much more difficult.

TASK ESTIMATING

Estimating the work associated with each task can be a challenging endeavor. It can be time consuming, especially for large projects or particularly complex tasks. Management often wants the PM to provide estimates quickly, and it can seem like there is not enough time to adequately consider the time or resources needed to fulfill each task in the plan.

Common approaches to estimating include:

- Analogous or top-down estimating – Using the actual costs of tasks in an previous, similar project as a basis for estimating the costs of an upcoming project.
- Bottom-up estimating – Estimating individual tasks at the lowest level of detail and summing them to get a total project estimate.
- Parametric modeling – Using project characteristics (or parameters) in a mathematical model to estimate project costs.
- Computerized estimating – Using digital tools, like spreadsheets and project management software.

Tasks have several dimensions to consider when estimating and developing a project plan, including:

- Duration
- Interrelationships
- Resource availability
- Costs.

Pragmatic PM Rule #24: Project tasks have four critical dimensions: duration, interrelationships, resource availability, and costs.

Task Duration

The first task dimension to consider is its duration. For example, it might take a software developer with expert skills 25 hours to develop an XML schema for a system interface. That duration can be derived from analogous projects, developer input, or from other expert sources. In this case, work equates to the duration of the effort needed to satisfy the requirement.

Although some people prefer to estimate work in days, weeks, or even months, for planning purposes the best estimate of work duration is given in hours. The PM can spread hours across a schedule, accounting for variable work schedules and productivity levels specific to the abilities of each team member.

If a PM gives estimates in days or weeks, it is unclear what those figures mean exactly. During the typical eight-hour workday, for example, the average worker is productive for 80 percent of those eight hours—6.4 hours—when accounting for vacation, sick leave, childcare emergencies, basic administrative overhead, and so on. By that logic, eight work hours would take approximately one and one-third days.

The critical path is the network of essential tasks that have the longest collective duration in a project. In other words, fulfilling that network of tasks determines when the entire project itself can be completed—it represents the shortest amount of time needed to complete the project.

In theory, managing the tasks on the critical path means managing the tasks that most directly drive the project toward completion. All other networks of tasks have slack or extra time built into them and so require less-intensive management. In practice, most PMs prefer to focus on the full project plan. But it is certainly a best practice to at least periodically review the critical path to ensure delays or changes impeding the critical path are addressed.

Task Interrelationships

The second task dimension to consider is its interrelationships with other tasks. All tasks are linked to at least one other task in some way. For example, some tasks must finish before others can start. Or it might be efficient to start several tasks simultaneously. It might be equally efficient for other tasks to finish simultaneously.

Task interrelationships form a network along which the project progresses from beginning to end (Figure 4-1).

The tasks outlined in Figure 4-1 are part of the project plan displayed as a Gantt chart in Figure 4-2.

Resource Availability

The third task dimension to consider relates to the resources necessary to complete the task. As described in Chapter 3, resource requirements are determined by identifying the skill sets needed for the project; defining the work required for each skill set; converting the work into time

Figure 4-1 Sample Network of Tasks

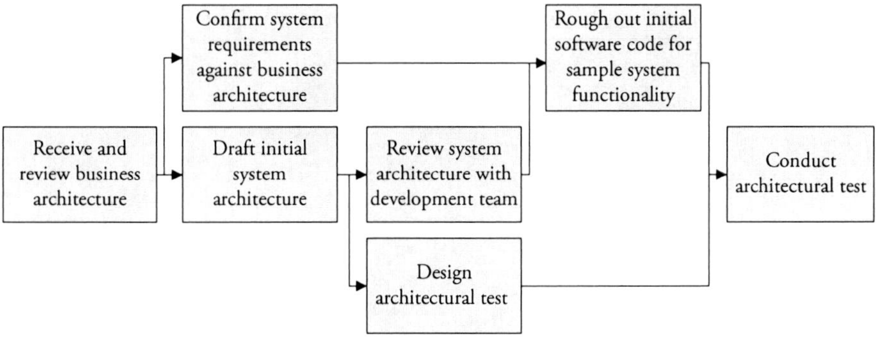

Receive and review business architecture

Confirm system requirements against business architecture

Draft initial system architecture

Review system architecture with development team

Design architectural test

Rough out initial software code for sample system functionality

Conduct architectural test

Figure 4-2 Sample Gantt Chart

ID	Task Name	Resource Names	March S S M T W T F S S M T W T F S S
1	Receive and review business architecture	Architect - J. Jones	
2	Confirm system requirements against business architecture	Business Analyst - A. Pratt	
3	Draft initial system architecture	Architect - J. Jones	
4	Review system architecture with development team	Architect - J. Jones, Developer 1 - E. Smith, Developer 2 - K. White	
5	Design architectural test	Architect - J. Jones	
6	Rough out initial software code for sample system functionality	Developer 1- E. Smith, Developer 2 - K. White	
7	Conduct architectural test	Architect - J. Jones, Developer 1 - E. Smith, Developer 2 - K. White	

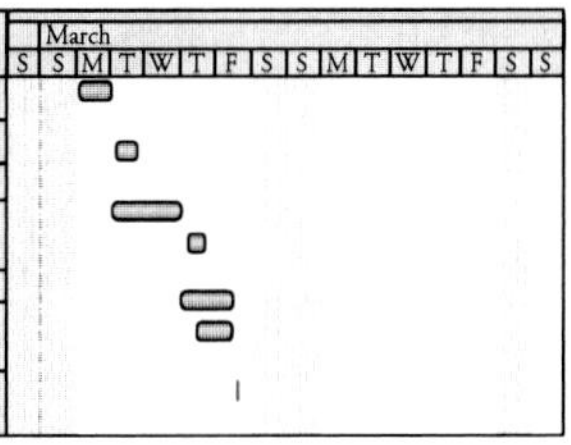

packages that can be assigned to resources; and scheduling resources to align with the required work.

In the schedule shown in Figure 4-2, assume that the architect is available to work only six hours per day and the two software developers are each available to work eight hours per day. One business analyst is also available, but only for four hours per day. Factoring in the average resource productivity level of 80 percent, the actual hours anticipated from each resource per day are outlined in Figure 4-3:

Figure 4-3 Projected Resource Availability

Resource Type	Availability	Factor for Actual Productivity	Anticipated Availability per Day
Architect	Six hours/day	80%	4.8 hours/day
Developer #1	Eight hours/day	80%	6.4 hours/day
Developer #2	Eight hours/day	80%	6.4 hours/day
Business Analyst	Four hours/day	80%	3.2 hours/day

Figure 4-4 Sample Gantt Chart Adjusted for Resource Availability

ID	Task Name	Resource Names
1	Receive and review business architecture	Architect - J. Jones
2	Confirm system requirements against business architecture	Business Analyst - A. Pratt
3	Draft initial system architecture	Architect - J. Jones
4	Review system architecture with development team	Architect - J. Jones, Developer 1 - E. Smith, Developer 2 - K. White
5	Design architectural test	Architect - J. Jones
6	Rough out initial software code for sample system functionality	Developer 1- E. Smith, Developer 2 - K. White
7	Conduct architectural test	Architect - J. Jones, Developer 1 - E. Smith, Developer 2 - K. White

March
S S M T W T F S S M T W T F S S

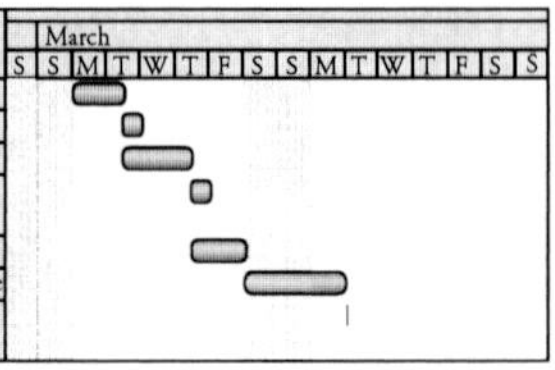

Assigning each of the workers to their respective tasks and factoring in each worker's availability impacts the schedule—the schedule now comprises two weeks instead of one week (Figure 4-4).

Task Costs

The fourth and final task dimension to consider is its cost. Resources cost money. Project managers must assign a cost—generally figured in resource wages per hour—to each task in the project plan. Project planning software tools assign input resource costs to each task and calculate total costs for the project, making it easier for PMs to make budget estimates.

MILESTONES

A milestone is a point in time on a project plan that is typically not associated with any specific work task. Instead, milestones are schedule markers that can indicate the end of a project phase, a go/no-go decision, or any other point where the project needs to pause for an assessment of some kind. Effective project managers use milestones judiciously for each of these purposes, and in general, milestones are great for parsing up project plans.

SCALING THE PROJECT PLAN

Project plans come in various formats, lengths, and levels of complexity, depending on the project. Effective project managers should tailor the project plan accordingly.

Pragmatic PM Rule #25: Scale the project plan to meet the project's needs.

The Napkin Approach

Sometimes a simple sketch is all that's needed as a project plan. Think of a very small project, such as organizing a celebratory picnic for a successful project team. The team in charge of the picnic is a small group of three volunteers. They envision a potluck picnic lunch in a park near a lake on a sunny day, where their coworkers can relax with each other and with their families. Over coffee, the picnic committee sketches things out on a napkin. The committee leader assigns one person the responsibility of organizing the pot-luck and another the responsibility of reserving space at a local community park. The leader will tackle the issue of entertainment and novelty awards to recognize each attendee's contribution to the successful project. A week later the picnic is held, and the weather cooperates by providing a warm, sunny day. The gathering is a great success.

In this instance, the risk to the organization was low, and the complexity of the project was also low. Very little project management was required to bring the project to a successful conclusion.

The Detailed Project Plan

On the other hand, basing the success or failure of a million-dollar project on a work plan sketched hastily on a napkin is not advisable. Generally, as the project's complexity grows, so does the content and expansiveness of the project plan. As the business investment in a project increases, so does the associated risk and the need to manage those risks. Developing a comprehensive and increasingly detailed project plan is a good way to address risk and protect the investment.

Constructing a project plan for a large, complex project can be arduous, time-consuming work. Carefully considering the project's vision, objectives, requirements, and related tasks allows the project team to thoroughly understand the work each task entails, and it reduces project risk, making such careful considerations well worth the effort.

Pragmatic PM Rule #26: A small project may require only a simple sketch as a project plan; a large, complex, expensive project may require a highly detailed project plan.

It is common for organizations—especially organizations not accustomed to managing projects—to feel tempted to skip project planning in favor of getting directly to the work. Unfortunately, many project management practitioners have reinforced this tendency by encouraging the organizations they work for to engage in overzealous project planning processes.

A few years ago, a public-sector agency commissioned a feasibility study to identify the best automated solution for a newly chartered organization providing support to healthcare beneficiaries. The goal of the project was to identify the business need the new system would support; identify several alternative approaches for satisfying that business need; select the best alternative as the automated solution; and identify the related costs and benefits provided by the solution. The results of the feasibility study would impact only one organization, and anticipated costs totaled approximately $200,000.

The project plan included the following work breakdown structure:

1	Conduct Feasibility Study – Phase I
1.1	Initiate Project
1.1.1	Develop Project Charter
1.1.2	Conduct State Review and Solicit Comments
1.1.3	Develop Project Plan
1.1.4	Develop Project Schedule
1.1.5	Conduct State Review and Solicit Comments
1.1.6	Conduct Kick-Off Meeting
1.1.7	Develop Deliverable Expectation Document
1.1.8	Conduct State Review and Solicit Comments

1.2 Gather Data

1.2.1 Gather User Information

1.2.2 Perform Market Analysis

1.3 Perform Needs Assessment

1.3.1 Workshop 1 – Constraints and Architecture

1.3.2 Workshop 2 – Business Needs and Objectives

1.3.3 Workshop 3 – Findings Validation

1.3.4 Prepare Deliverable – Background Needs Assessment and Objectives

1.3.5 Conduct State Review and Solicit Comments

1.4 Conduct Requirements Analysis

1.4.1 Workshop 1 – Functional Requirements

1.4.2 Workshop 2 – Technical Requirements

1.4.3 Workshop 3 – Findings Validation

1.4.4 Prepare Deliverable – Requirements and Definitions

1.4.5 Conduct State Review and Solicit Comments

1.5 Conduct Alternatives Analysis

1.5.1 Research Vendors and State Alternatives

1.5.2 Conduct Detailed Analysis

1.5.3 Workshop – Alternatives Analysis

1.5.4 Prepare Deliverable

1.5.4.1 Discuss Major Alternatives

1.5.4.2 Conduct Cost/Benefit Analysis

1.5.5 Conduct State Review and Solicit Comments

1.6 Conduct Proposed-Solution Analysis

1.6.1 Conduct Proposed-Solution Assessment

1.6.2 Workshop 1 – Proposed-Solution Implementation Approach

1.6.3 Workshop 2 – Proposed-Solution Risk Assessment

1.6.4 Prepare Deliverable – Feasibility Study Core Elements

1.6.5 Conduct State Review and Solicit Comments

1.6.6 Prepare Formal Feasibility Study Report

1.6.7 Conduct State Review and Solicit Comments

1.6.8 Develop Systems Migration Approach

1.6.9 Workshop 3 – Overall Systems Migration Approach

2 Request Proposals – Phase II

2.1 Develop Procurement Strategy

2.1.1 Develop Procurement Strategy

2.1.2 Conduct State Review and Solicit Comments

2.1.3 Develop Evaluation Strategy

2.1.4 Conduct State Review and Solicit Comments

2.1.5 Perform Risk Assessment

2.1.6 Conduct State Review and Solicit Comments

2.1.7 Develop Model Contract

2.1.8 Conduct State Review and Solicit Comments

2.1.9 Workshop – Confirm Procurement Strategy

2.1.10 Update Phase I Work Plan and Project Charter

2.1.11 Conduct State Review and Solicit Comments

2.1.12 Prepare Deliverable – Request for Proposals

2.1.13 Conduct State Review and Solicit Comments

2.2 Develop Request for Proposal Document

2.2.1 Draft Major Sections of Request for Proposals

2.2.2 Conduct State Review and Solicit Comments

2.2.3 Develop Final Request for Proposals

2.2.4 Conduct State Review and Solicit Comments

2.3 Develop Evaluation Tools

2.3.1	Develop Assessment Criteria
2.3.2	Conduct State Review and Solicit Comments
2.3.3	Develop Proposal Evaluation Workbook
2.3.4	Conduct State Review and Solicit Comments
2.4	Conduct Evaluation Training Session
2.4.1	Develop Training Materials
2.4.2	Conduct Training
3	Manage Project – Phase III
3.1	Write Monthly Progress Reports
3.2	Conduct Weekly Project Team Meetings
3.3	Conduct Executive Steering Committee Meetings
3.4	Write Project Closure Report
3.5	Close Phases I and II

A young project manager was assigned to the project. She had recently assisted with a large, highly complex IT project that had proved difficult for the organization and was nearly shut down because of mismanagement. This experience shaped her approach to the feasibility project and compelled her to rewrite the project plan outlined above to include more than 400 work elements broken down by the hour.

Driven by the near failure of her last project, this young PM was determined to manage each step of the feasibility project in minute detail. She brought together a talented team of technical and business experts and hired a highly qualified consulting firm to conduct the actual study. She also hired an external quality assurance (QA) analyst to provide oversight consultation to the project sponsor and to advise the project manager.

Determined to succeed, the PM developed a new project plan without requesting input from her project team. Though the feasibility study was fairly simple, the PM created the type of minutely detailed, step-by-step project plan suitable for only the largest, most complex projects. She micromanaged every resource assigned to the project, regardless of their concerns that her excessive attention to detail was not necessary. She was observed berating her team members in public for inconsequential editorial mistakes on specifications that had no bearing on the final outcome of the project.

As a result, the project eventually ground to a halt. The project team lost motivation and interest in the project, finding excuses to work elsewhere in the organization and leaving the project manager stranded without support. Relatively simple deliverable reports went without finalization as a result of unnecessary criticisms. The PM ignored suggestions provided by the external QA analyst. When the QA analyst escalated those issues, the project sponsor removed the PM from the project and replaced her with another individual who managed to get the project moving forward again.

When projects appear to progress much slower than anticipated, it may be a result of over-planning. The importance of a good, well-considered project approach cannot be overstated. However, over-planning and insisting upon an unnecessary level of detail when a simpler approach might be appropriate can bog a project down and prematurely exhaust the project budget, leading to project failure.

An adequate, successful project plan is one that describes work packages in enough detail for the project team to know what needs to be done and to identify the resources required to complete the project successfully. As with all efforts in pragmatic project management, the goal is to determine the minimum amount of effort needed to deliver the maximum benefit for the project. Scale the project plan and planning efforts to meet the needs of the project (Figure 4-5).

All the content of the project plan must trace back to the project vision: Tasks trace to requirements; requirements trace to objectives; and objectives trace to the project vision issued by the project sponsor. Beginning with this tenet of traceability, the subsequent goal is always to provide enough information to enable the project team to complete the project successfully by progressing through tasks in a logical, sequential fashion.

There is no minimum number of tasks necessary to write a good project plan. The substance of the plan matters, not the number of tasks.

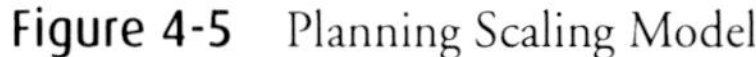

Figure 4-5 Planning Scaling Model

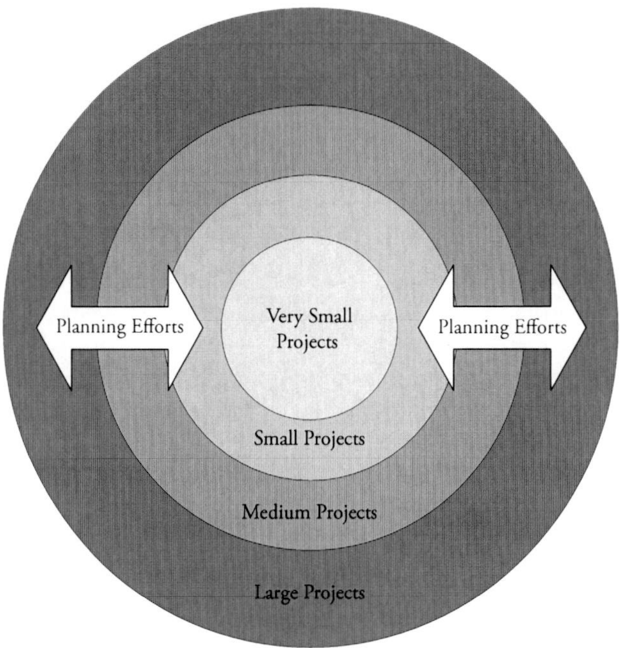

PROJECT PLANNING CHECKLIST

Description	Yes	No	N/A
Define the project vision.			
Define project objectives with approval from the project sponsor, and ensure objectives are traceable to the project vision statement.			
Define project requirements, and ensure requirements are traceable to project objectives.			
Define project tasks, and ensure tasks are traceable to project requirements.			
Estimate the duration of each task.			
Define the sequence and interrelationships of all tasks.			
Estimate resource availability for each task.			
Estimate the cost of each task.			
Create milestones to indicate the end of a project phase or any other point at which the project needs to pause for an assessment of some kind.			

Chapter 5

Pragmatic PM Element #4: Project Issue Management

Overlooking project issue management can cause a great deal of trouble. As a project management process, issue management is relatively simple, straightforward, and quite beneficial. It is an important essential element of pragmatic project management.

Issues of various types and complexity come up on projects every day. Each issue has common characteristics the PM can identify and monitor, such as the source of the issue, the date the issue was identified, the form of action taken to address the issue, the resource assigned to address the issue, and the date the issue was resolved.

In its simplest form, project issue management is a two-step process involving questions and answers. Someone asks a question, and someone else answers the question. Issues are matters that could potentially impact the project, and issue management means managing and tracking those matters to resolution. When a question or concern is raised about some aspect of a project, it should be clarified, described to the right people, and tracked or resolved.

Consider, for example, hikers about to undertake a day-trip into the hills. One hiker asks about the availability of water; the other tells the hiker about several water sources along the way and says that they should each bring a canteen to store water in between the sources. This suggestion is a planned resolution to the issue of water availability.

Things get a little more complicated when a resolution to the issue is not readily available. Consider a different set of hikers who are not familiar with the route and do not know whether water is available along the way. One hiker asks about water, but neither accepts responsibility for finding an answer. Instead, they each assume the other will resolve the issue, and neither one worries about finding water along the way. This unresolved issue could have a serious impact on the hikers.

Successful project managers track unresolved issues until a resolution is reached and communicated to the party who raised the issue, so everyone understands the issue and its resolution. Project teams that don't formally track issues can overlook or forget them, only to see them arise again later in the project—e.g., as a late-phase change in scope or as a user who refuses to accept the project deliverable. Mismanaged issues eventually consume an inordinate amount of time and resources, distracting the team significantly and making project success less likely.

Any number of issues can arise over the course of a project. Issues are typically raised by project team members, project sponsors, end-users, or other stakeholders, and most can be resolved on the spot with a simple yes or no answer or a brief explanation. The toughest issues are usually raised by people; e.g., when someone approaches the PM and inquires about an aspect of the project. When the project is moving at full pace and there is hardly enough time to finish the work already within the project's scope, such inquiries can cause worry. Taking the time to address inquiries and suggestions, however, can facilitate aspects of the project in unexpected ways.

Most issues address one or more project requirements. When a requirement is not fulfilled, or when it appears as though a project might not satisfy a particular requirement, a project stakeholder is likely to raise the issue. Concerns raised might provide valuable insight into a specific requirement or set of requirements at risk. At the very least, the issue will signal a need to clarify expectations or provide a status update to particular stakeholders.

Unresolved issues often evolve into something greater than a simple stakeholder concern. Left untended, issues can morph into change requests submitted late in the project lifecycle, when the cost of implementing changes is substantially greater than in earlier phases. Unresolved issues can also become risks threatening project success. If a primary beneficiary of the project deliverable does not share a consistent set of expectations with the project team, the beneficiary is likely to find the deliverable unacceptable at the end of the project.

To avoid potential difficulties of this type, project managers must document issues as they arise and track them to resolution.

Pragmatic PM Rule #27: Every project has issues; manage them or be managed *by* them.

Figure 5-1 shows a typical project issue management workflow.

The Pareto principle, which states that 80 percent of effects are generated by just 20 percent of causes, commonly applies to project issue management. According to this principle, only 20 percent of project issues cause 80 percent of the effects that have a relatively significant impact on the project. These issues require more work to resolve and deserve more attention. The other 80 percent of issues are caused by relatively minor circumstances and are fairly easy to resolve.

Pragmatic PM Rule #28: Most issues are fairly easy to resolve; only a small percentage will require more work to resolve and deserve more attention.

Issue management involves escalating information about issues to the proper level of management so any urgent decisions can be made with authority, and the project can move on from that issue to the next. The

Figure 5-1 Project Issue Management Workflow

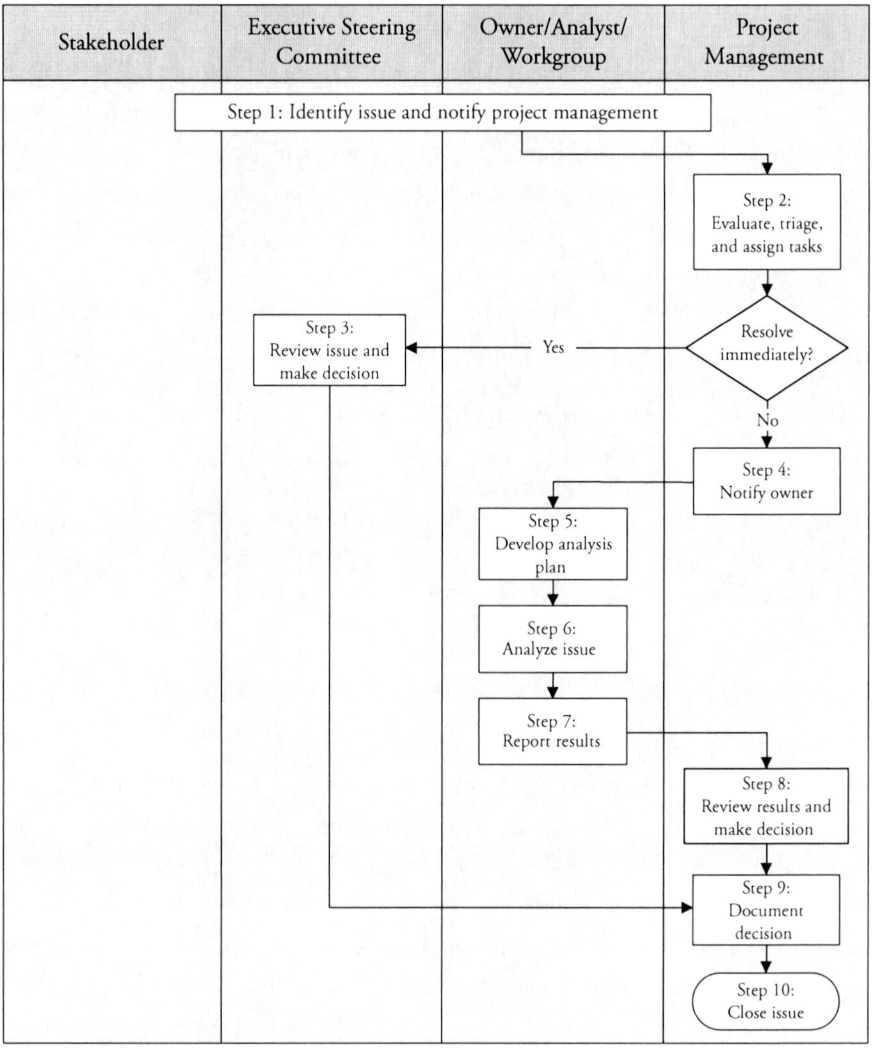

length of time it takes to resolve priority issues is a key indicator of the effectiveness of the PM and his or her team and an important predictor of project success. [2]

[2] The Standish Group International, *CHAOS Summary 2009: The 10 Laws of CHAOS* (Boston: The Standish Group International, Inc., 2009), pp. 1–3.

Pragmatic PM Rule #29: The length of time it takes to resolve priority issues is a key indicator of the effectiveness of the PM and his or her team and an important predictor of project success.

THE ISSUE TRACKING LOG

Documenting issues in an issue tracking log is a best practice used to record issues that are not resolved as a matter of course during meetings, discussions, basic design reviews, and so on. Issues that are not immediately resolved—e.g., within a couple of hours—should be recorded in the tracking log.

An issue tracking log typically contains the following information:

- A unique identifying issue number
- A brief description of the issue
- The name of the person(s) who raised the issue
- The phase(s) of the project affected by the issue
- Who the issue was assigned to for resolution
- Issue status (e.g., open, closed)
- A brief description of how the issue was resolved
- The date the issue was opened
- The date the issue was closed.

Issue tracking logs should not be complex. While software applications are available to help project managers tackle issues, in many cases a simple spreadsheet will suffice. Figure 5-2 shows a simple, straightforward way to format a tracking log.

The issue tracking log provides a punch list of things to resolve before the project can be completed. The project team can address stakeholder questions and communicate them to the appropriate parties, managing expectations and providing valuable information, all of which enables the team to deliver a better product or service.

The log also provides less obvious but equally important value as a repository for important project information. Issues tend to recur throughout the project lifecycle. Sometimes the issue tracking log will reveal that the

Figure 5-2 Sample Issue Tracking Log

Issue No.	Issue Description	Submitted By	Affected Project Phase(s)	Assigned To	Status	Issue Resolution	Date Opened	Date Closed
1	Project manager may be replaced after conclusion of project authorization phase	X. Ross, PMP	Project planning phase and later phases	Project sponsor	Closed	New PM hired and brought on for knowledge transfer prior to departure of current PM	June 4, 2010	July 1, 2010
2	Vendor to provide foundation materials was unable to provide sufficient aggregate material in gravel	M. Builder, CMM	Planning and execution phases	Technical lead	Open		June 15, 2010	
3	County inspectors may change building codes applicable to framing and electrical wiring	M. Builder, CMM	Planning and execution phases	Electrical engineer	Open		June 17, 2010	
4								
5								
6								

project team improperly dealt with an issue initially, causing the issue to recur. Without a well-kept issue tracking log, the team could waste time reworking issues repeatedly.

Consider, for example, an important architectural issue addressed early during an IT project. Several months—or even years—later, a question is raised about the same issue. Without an issue tracking log, the project team would have to dig through specification documents to find an answer. Even though the team might have to do this in any case, an issue tracking log would identify the original issue and the specific action taken to resolve the issue. This information would at least aid the team's investigation process, allowing it to move forward much more efficiently.

Pragmatic PM Rule #30: Keep an issue tracking log to track, manage, and resolve issues efficiently.

THE ISSUE MANAGEMENT FORM

Sometimes issues take more than a brief discussion or notation to fully understand and appreciate. Highly technical information is often complex and challenging. In certain cases, the project team must document issues in greater detail than that typically provided by a simple issue tracking log. An issue management form provides more information about the issue and its resolution, and it typically requires a signature from the project sponsor to ensure he or she is made fully aware of highly complex issues.

Pragmatic PM Rule #31: Describe complex issues in an issue management form, and record less-detailed information about the issue in the issue management log.

Issue management forms should not be overly complex; excessive bureaucracy can discourage project team members from completing the form and could result in issues documented poorly or not at all. Instead, the issue management form should simply provide sufficient space for the author to elaborate on the issue without excessive verbosity (Figure 5-3).

Figure 5-3 Issue Management Form

<table>
<tr><td>Client:</td><td colspan="3"></td></tr>
<tr><td>Project Name:</td><td></td><td>Date of Report:</td><td></td></tr>
<tr><td>Issue #:</td><td></td><td>Submitted By:</td><td></td></tr>
<tr><td>Project Phase Impacted:</td><td colspan="3"></td></tr>
<tr><td colspan="4">Issue Description</td></tr>
<tr><td colspan="4"></td></tr>
<tr><td colspan="4">Action Taken</td></tr>
<tr><td colspan="4"></td></tr>
<tr><td>Date Resolved:</td><td colspan="3"></td></tr>
<tr><td>Project Sponsor Signature:</td><td colspan="3"></td></tr>
</table>

As with all aspects of pragmatic project management, the rule is to apply minimum effort to yield maximum gain for the project. Use only the documentation necessary to ensure that the issue can be understood, communicated, and resolved.

PRIORITIZING ISSUES

When the project team encounters hundreds of issues over time, it can be difficult to decide which issues to address first—especially when team members are otherwise engaged in scheduled project work throughout the workday. Managing issues can seem like just one more burden needing attention, and addressing the issue may or may not provide lasting value other than appeasing the stakeholder who raised the issue.

So how can PMs differentiate important issues from less-meaningful ones? As in all cases where workload exceeds capacity, the answer is by prioritizing.

Pragmatic PM Rule #32: When numerous issues need attention, prioritize and address the most important issues first.

The beauty of a well-assembled project team is the diversity of talents and perspectives it makes available to the PM when difficult problems arise. The collective experience and talents of team members can go a long way toward resolving many issues rather quickly. Bring the team together to review the issue tracking log and prioritize issues. First, address issues that could be resolved immediately or fairly easily. Then briefly discuss each remaining issue and describe its relative importance to the project. From there, assign priority to each issue and give it a priority value in the issue tracking log (Figure 5-4).

Prioritizing issues is a critical aspect of issue management. The number of issues identified and managed over the course of a project's lifecycle can be daunting, yet the risk associated with not managing issues appropriately can be significant. Effectively managing large numbers of issues means prioritizing them so limited resources and time are spent on only the most important issues involving the most project risk. Prioritizing the issues makes it easier for the project manager and the rest of the project team to focus on high-priority issues that have the greatest potential effect on the project.

The most important issues to address are those affecting project scope, schedule, or cost, which are more likely to evolve into change requests that place the fundamental success of the project at risk. These issues are generally given a "1" priority value.

Consider an IT project commissioned to provide a new financial accounting system. The project team has worked with the client's accounting department to develop and document the new system's requirements.

Figure 5-4 Sample Issue Tracking Log with Priority Values

Issue No.	Priority Value	Issue Description	Submitted By	Affected Project Phase(s)	Issue Resolution	Assigned To	Status	Date Opened	Date Closed
1	2	Project manager may be replaced after conclusion of project authorization phase	X. Ross, PMP	Project planning phase and later phases	Project sponsor	Closed	New PM hired and brought on for knowledge transfer prior to departure of current PM	June 4, 2010	July 1, 2010
2	1	Vendor to provide foundation materials was unable to provide sufficient aggregate material in gravel	M. Builder, CMM	Planning and execution phases	Technical lead	Open		June 15, 2010	
3	2	County inspectors may change building codes applicable to framing and electrical wiring	M. Builder, CMM	Planning and execution phases	Electrical engineer	Open		June 17, 2010	
4									
5									

Software developers identify an appropriate accounts payable software package and an accounts receivable management software package and integrate them with a general ledger module customized by the technical team. During the initial testing of the integrated system, an accountant reviews the software and indicates that the accounts payable software package is out of date; a more recent edition exists and has greater functionality.

The PM notes the accountant's concern and documents it in the project's issue log. He summarizes the issue; records the name of the accountant who raised the concern; and assigns the issue to the technical team leader to investigate, indicating that the issue addresses the accounts payable component of the financial accounting system. The PM notes that the issue could impact project schedule and cost and so makes resolving the issue a top priority, giving it a "1" priority value.

If the project team does its job well, it will resolve the issue by ensuring that the appropriate version of the accounts payable software package will be integrated into the financial accounting system. Once this information is confirmed, the PM can note the resolution in the issues log and notify the accountant who raised the issue.

Issues of lower priority—those given a priority value of "2"—impact aspects of the project other than scope, schedule, or cost, but they can still have a meaningful impact on the project and should be addressed. These issues might involve the project's political environment or logistics. For example, if facility resources or equipment are available on only a limited basis, changes in that availability might impact project execution without directly impacting project scope, schedule, or cost.

New construction projects involving the development of public facilities often attract significant public attention. Because the public is often interested in how the government spends tax revenue and because the public has an interest in public facilities, these stakeholders often raise issues that can have an impact on projects. Issue management in these cases can be a real challenge.

Consider a project to build a new elementary school. The funding provided for the new school comes from a variety of sources, including governmental appropriations, collections from the school district's community, and grants. During the course of construction, area politicians and community leaders will likely monitor exactly how those funds are spent during the project. As a result, the project manager's staff receives a fairly constant flow of calls requesting information about the project and asking for tours of the construction site.

As issues, none of these requests are likely to directly impact the project's scope, schedule, or cost. However, if the PM does not record, monitor, and respond to each issue in a timely manner, it can lead to all sorts of distractions. The concerns of the politicians and community leaders are important issues that the PM should take seriously. The PM should document each issue in the issues log and track it to resolution when the requested information or tour of the construction site are provided.

Low-priority issues—those given a priority value of "3"—create background noise for project team members that might be bothersome but has little or no material impact on the project if left unaddressed. Low-priority issues are lingering concerns related to minor day-to-day events that have little significant impact on the project as a whole but might benefit from the project team's attention, time permitting.

For example, an informal information request from a weekly newspaper for a human interest article about a project conducted by a nonprofit service group might be considered a low-priority issue. Providing the information might benefit the project, but the PM could elect to respond to the request only when time permits, rather than make it a higher priority. The likelihood that the issue will evolve into something that negatively impacts the project is small. Even if the PM is unable to respond to the request for information, it is likely the newspaper will simply lose interest in the article and move on to other, more pressing subjects.

In any case, the PM should still document the issue in the issues log, not only to keep track of all issues, but also because if time permits, someone representing the project could respond to the newspaper's request for information, which could potentially benefit the project in some small way. Another reason why it is important for the PM to document all issues in a log is because any issue can change in priority and become more important over time.

As the previous examples demonstrate, the issue management log has many valuable functions. The log is a useful tool for documenting both simple and complex issues. When used with the issue management form, the issue log becomes a repository of active and resolved issues of varying priority and can help project team members gauge how best to manage issues to resolution. An issue management log also helps the project team stay focused. Project managers who bring the issue log to project team meetings can use it as a point of departure for discussion, to review open issues, assess their priority, and assign action items.

SCOPE-CHANGE REQUESTS

Ignoring issues instead of managing them carefully can cost the project team a lot of time, frustration, and money. When left alone, issues can develop into significant project risks or scope-change requests that can have a significant effect on the final project deliverable.

Pragmatic PM Rule #33: Carefully manage issues as they arise to preclude costly scope changes late in the project lifecycle.

Scope change can be relatively painless and inexpensive early in the planning phase of a project. The same change can be extremely costly if it arises later in the project, when the deliverable designs are final and construction is well underway. Carefully managing issues as they arise can help preclude costly scope changes late in the project lifecycle.

Scope-change requests require modifications to the project deliverable. The term *scope* simply defines what the project will and will not entail. The project manager determines what the project will entail by defining the best way to satisfy the project vision and objectives. Whenever the project scope changes, a subsequent impact on cost and schedule will occur. If project cost and schedule estimates are accurate initially, a subsequent change in scope will cause a change in the work needed to satisfy that scope. Work changes will affect the original cost and schedule estimates accordingly.

Consider a school construction project. The approved scope for the original project includes classrooms, a theater arts and music room, a cafeteria, a multipurpose room, and administrative offices. Project work, cost, and schedule estimates are drafted and approved accordingly, and the initial design process begins.

Halfway through the design process, the state government offers a grant to use for a school swimming pool and fitness area. Meanwhile, local parents lobby for a new football stadium, as well. The PM gives estimates for the additional work and determines the grant is sufficient to cover the cost of a pool and a small weight room, but not a football stadium. The additional work will add 12 months to the original construction schedule. The modified scope statement now includes the pool and the weight room, but excludes the football stadium.

As this example demonstrates, stakeholders often present scope-change requests without considering how the changes could impact project costs and schedule. Therefore, the PM must "protect" the project scope by considering each scope-change request carefully and agreeing to changes in scope only when schedule and cost estimates are adjusted as necessary.

Specific tools can help ensure that scope remains stable through the life of a project. The first is a scope-change request form. This form identifies the nature of the change request, how the change could impact project scope, and how the change could impact project cost and schedule. The form also typically provides a space for the project sponsor to write a review of the change request, since it is the project sponsor who ultimately must pay for the changes. Figure 5-5 presents a sample scope-change request form.

Like issues, it is important that change requests be tracked over time to ensure that they receive an appropriate review. Many projects are audited during and after project completion. A change-control log can be helpful for ensuring that changes to project budget and schedule are auditable over time. Figure 5-6 presents a sample change-control log.

The procedures used to document and manage change requests should be published as a change-control plan. This plan should be made available

Figure 5-5 Sample Scope-Change Request Form

Project Name :		**Date :**	
Change Request # :		**Submitted By :**	
Description of Change :			
Motivation for Change :			
Cost Impact :			
Schedule Impact :			
Scope Change Approved or Disapproved :			
Reason for Approval or Disapproval :			
Project Sponsor Signature :			

Figure 5-6 Sample Change-Control Log

Change Request #	Description of Change	Cost Impact	Schedule Impact	Approved or Disapproved	Date Resolved
2011-1	Add swimming pool and fitness room	+$1.4 million	+12 months	Approved	1/15/2011
2011-2	Remove stage area in multipurpose room	-$150, 000	-Two months	Approved	2/14/2011
2011-3					
2011-4					

to project team members and interested stakeholders to ensure that they know how to submit change requests and how change requests will be documented and reviewed.

RISK MANAGEMENT

Project risks are events that might happen in the future and if so, might impact the project. Risks may be positive or negative. A positive risk might benefit the project if it comes to fruition. Project managers seldom actively deal with positive risks. Instead, PMs are generally too busy figuring out how to best deal with the risks that might negatively impact the project.

When issues evolve into risks, they assume a new level of importance, especially if the risk could impact project scope, schedule, or cost. Common risks of this type include the need to conduct additional project work, modify project plans, or pay more to accommodate changes.

Project managers must consider the probability of each risk actually occurring. A risk is something that might happen in the future; it is uncertain whether the risk event will actually come to pass or not. The probability of a risk manifesting during the project lifecycle can be determined by the project team through the use of computer simulations, expert consultation, experience, or simply the project manager's best judgment.

A risk involved in planning a community fair, for example, is the 30 percent chance that weather conditions might prevent the vendor providing carnival rides from setting up in the usual location. If this happens, the fair committee will need to rent space at a commercial parking lot for an additional $1,000.

Risks, like the issues they often spring from, can be numerous and difficult to manage. One strategy for managing a high number of risks is to prioritize them according to probability and potential impact. For example, a risk that is highly likely to occur and could have a significant impact on the project might be assigned a priority value of "1." A risk less likely to occur and with less potential impact might be assigned a low priority value, like "2" or "3."

The culture and experience of the sponsoring organization will affect the way it assigns priority to project risks. The community fair committee, for example, might consider a potential impact of $1,000 as a significant risk, irrespective of its probability. An aircraft manufacturer managing projects worth millions of dollars, however, might consider a $1,000 risk negligible and so would assign it low priority among other risks.

Given the variety of approaches to risk, the PM must understand how the sponsoring organization assigns high, medium, and low priority to risks. One organization might give high priority only to risks with a 90 percent likelihood of occurrence. Another organization that is less risk-tolerant might give high priority to all risks with more than a 50 percent likelihood of occurrence. Whatever the rating scheme, if risks are classified with high, medium, and low priority ratings, the PM and the project team must understand how those ratings are determined for the risk classifications to serve any real purpose.

Risks are commonly identified in a risk management log. Like the issue management log, the risk management log defines and documents risks and acts as a point of departure for team meeting discussions and when developing strategies to mitigate potential risks. As always, the objective is to apply minimum effort to achieve maximum project gain. Figure 5-7

Figure 5-7 Sample Risk Management Log with Priority Value

Risk #	Priority	Description	Impact	Likelihood	Strategy	Action Plan	Assigned To	Current Status	Last Update
1	2	The desired aggregate for the foundation concrete will be discontinued by the vendor, and a second vendor will be needed.	$40,000 in cost; two weeks in schedule	30%	Mitigate	Identify backup vendor in advance of contract award. Pre-position orders for aggregate and file in case of need.	Project site supervisor	Open	10/6/10
2	1	City council members consider this a high-visibility project. Visits from council members and their constituents on a monthly basis are likely.	$40,000 in cost; occurs throughout project	90%	Mitigate	Hire a communications manager on a half-time basis to stay in touch with local politicians and resolve their concerns through proactive communications management.	Project manager	Open	10/1/10
3									
4									

presents a simple risk management log that would likely suffice for most small and medium-sized projects. More elaborate software tools are available to help project teams manage risks associated with large, complex projects.

When managed well and resolved early in the project lifecycle, issues affecting project scope, schedule, or cost are less likely to evolve into scope changes or risks. The PM must manage the expectations of those who raise issues and work proactively to resolve issues as soon as possible.

For small projects, a well-documented issue management log may be sufficient to record issues. Small projects typically require less risk management than larger, more complex projects, where the project team is likely to confront a greater number of issues and thus will produce more extensive documentation. For large, complex projects, processes used by the project team to identify, assess, document, and manage risks should be documented in a brief risk management plan. This plan should clearly define the team's risk management responsibilities, including how to identify and respond to project risks.

ESCALATING ISSUES

No one has more at stake in a project than the sponsoring organization. This is why some project sponsors insist on knowing about certain types of issues as they arise and participating in important decision-making activities to address key issues.

Every project team has a hierarchy that begins on top with the project sponsor and works down to the administrative clerks (Figure 5-8). Effective issue management requires each member of the project team to understand his or her role in the decision-making hierarchy of the sponsoring organization. When issues arise that the project team cannot resolve, or when issues require decisions that only the project sponsor can make, the project team must escalate those issues to the project sponsor.

Each project team member is likely to encounter issues regularly. Most issues can be resolved easily without escalating the issue up the project hierarchy.

Figure 5-8 Simple Project Organization Chart

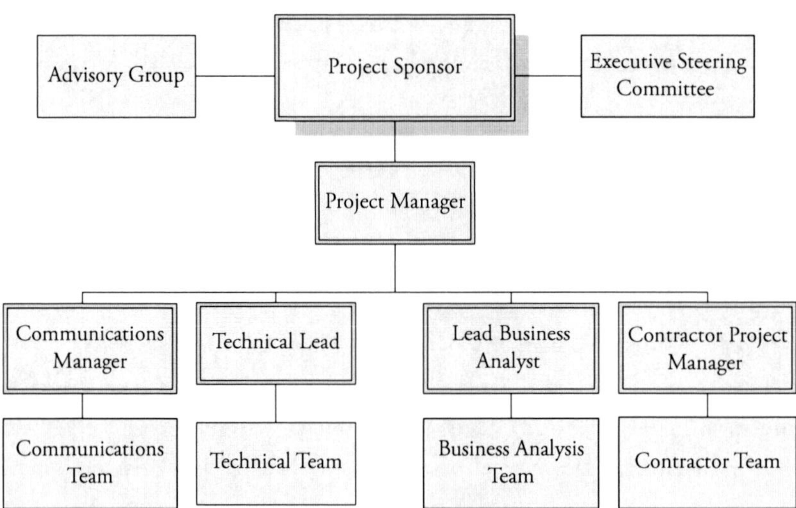

However, issues that cannot be resolved at lower levels will require escalation. Usually this means raising the issue to the lowest possible level where it can be effectively resolved. To ensure that the escalation process takes place in a logical, efficient manner, the PM should assign issue management roles and responsibilities to each project team member (Figure 5-9).

Certain issues should always be escalated to at least the project manager, if not also the project sponsor. Such issues include those affecting:

- Project scope, schedule, or cost
- The project team
- Key stakeholders
- External communications.

The project sponsor authorizes the project and makes final decisions regarding project scope, schedule, and cost. The project sponsor also typically makes final decisions regarding anything related to policy and anything with the potential to significantly impact the organization.

The project sponsor's willingness to take responsibility for decisions regarding significant issues greatly benefits the project manager because

Figure 5-9 Issue Management Roles and Responsibilities

Role	Responsibilities
Issue Identifier (e.g., stakeholder, team member, customer)	• Identifies issues • Documents issue information • Notifies project manager
Project Manager	• Evaluates issues • Defines issue priority • Escalates issues as necessary • Delegates issues to project team members • Monitors project team member issue analysis • Reviews issue-analysis results and makes decisions • Closes issues
Project Team Members – Issue Owners	• Analyzes issues to determine causes, effects • Develops alternative solutions • Recommends preferred solutions
Executive Steering Committee	• Reviews critical issues and recommends a decision to the project sponsor
Project Sponsor	• Has final decision-making authority for all decisions impacting the project's scope, schedule, and cost • Manages issues associated with specific, high-level stakeholders

it effectively relieves the PM from the need to entertain half-baked stakeholder issues or scope-change requests. If stakeholders know their issues will require analysis and approval from the project sponsor, they are often more reluctant to present anything but the most well-developed, important, and urgent issues. Without the involvement of the project sponsor, the PM could become inundated with off-the-cuff stakeholder ideas and issues, distracting him or her from the central task of managing the project team and successfully delivering the product or service.

Pragmatic PM Rule #34: The project sponsor makes final decisions on issues impacting project scope, schedule, or cost, and issues raised by key stakeholders.

DELEGATING ISSUES

All too often, project managers attempt to manage project issues all on their own. They may make an exception for the issues that the project sponsor elects to manage directly, but otherwise many PMs elect to address too many project issues.

Frequent and numerous project issues can result in an unmanageable situation for the PM, who relies on timely decision-making to maintain project momentum. The Standish Group identified timely decision-making by senior management as the number two factor affecting project success.[3] That statistic alone suggests how critical it is for the PM to not only escalate significant issues to the project sponsor, but also to delegate less significant issues to other, lower-ranking project team members as necessary. This expedites issue management by dispersing the effort to project team members at the appropriate level for timely resolution.

MANAGING STAKEHOLDER AND USER EXPECTATIONS

Successful project management is all about setting and managing expectations. Stakeholders most often raise issues when their expectations do not align with the actions of the project team. This makes it imperative for the PM to clearly identify stakeholders early in the project and closely manage their expectations. The PM must carefully communicate with stakeholders to identify and address their concerns early in the planning phase of the project lifecycle, when changes to project scope, schedule, and cost are easier and less costly to implement.

The old adage "pay now or pay later" applies in project management: Pay now by taking the time to address stakeholder concerns early in the project, or pay much more later on when forced to deal with stakeholder issues unresolved for too long.

---

[3] Jim Johnson, *My Life is Failure: 100 Things You Should Know to Be a Better Project Leader* (Boston: The Standish Group International, Inc., 2006), pp. 5–15.

SCALING THE WORK

As with all efforts in pragmatic project management, the goal is to apply minimum effort to achieve maximum gain for the project. Small projects typically require only a small amount of project issue management to keep the project on track and successfully deliver the product or service. For small and medium-sized projects, it may be sufficient to maintain a detailed issue management log to record issues and document their resolution, as long as the information in the log effectively tracks each issue from beginning to end.

Larger projects typically require more issue management and may require the PM to formalize the issue management process and expand it to include separate, specific risk management and scope management plans, processes, forms, and logs.

Years ago, I managed a simple $80,000 IT project using little more than scrap paper. The project team consisted of me and my technical lead, and our task was to implement a small software package. Because there were only two project team members, we conducted most of our project management tasks informally, working through the essential elements of pragmatic PM over coffee. Despite our informal approach, we successfully delivered the project on time and slightly under budget. Our simple efforts were sufficient.

The client was thrilled with our deliverable, and rather than close the project upon the initial release of the software, the client began asking rapid-fire questions about how to expand the new software to include more and more functionality. We found it increasingly difficult to keep track of the number of issues presented by the client. One morning, I gathered all the scraps of paper documenting project issues and entered the information into a quickly fabricated spreadsheet. I also began to request additional project resources.

The project team grew to include a dozen people. At the next project team meeting, we worked as a group to develop a formal process for managing issues. The process included referring all major issues to the project manager, documenting all issues, assigning issues to the appropriate team resource, and following up with the client to ensure that each issue was resolved to everyone's satisfaction.

As the list of issues grew, many evolved into scope-change requests. Over the next 12 months, the project grew in cost from its original $80,000 to more than $1 million. The issue management log documented each component of that cost growth as a scope-change request. The project team reviewed each scope-change request and ensured that the client approved each change, as well.

Project growth of this sort can be challenging to manage. When this particular project finally closed, for example, 360 issues were listed in the issue management log, including 50 scope-change requests. The project team joked that when the dust finally settled, the project had an issue for nearly every day of the year and a scope-change request for nearly every week of the year.

Large projects demand an investment in the time necessary to conduct careful issue management. When issues arise in rapid succession, informal documentation might not be sufficient. Without documenting and managing issues carefully, it can be easy to overlook important issues when the project is large, issues are extensive, and team members and stakeholders are numerous. Overlooking even one major issue can substantially impact the project.

Determining exactly how much issue management to apply to individual projects can be challenging. When should PMs formalize the issue management process or include separate risk and scope management plans? A good rule of thumb is to always use at least an informal spreadsheet or other tracking tool to document project issues that arise, regardless of project size or complexity. Even if the project remains small, a documented list of issues to refer to should at least help the PM avoid overlooking issues that might later impact the project deliverable.

If the project becomes substantially complex, having an issue management process in place will support the project. The project manager can apply risk and scope management as needed if substantial risks or scope-change requests arise.

Short of obsessing over individual issues to the point of distraction, it is difficult to over-manage issues. Issues arise in a number of ways, even during simple ad hoc discussions between end-users, project team members, stakeholders, and project managers. When resolved on the spot, it might not be necessary to document the issue unless there is reason to believe it could be important to reference the issue later. If not resolved on the spot, the PM should always document the issue and track it to resolution. The level of rigor the PM applies to the situation should correspond to the simple goal of resolving all project issues—either on the spot or through an approved issue management process.

Scope creep is the single most common symptom of mismanaged issues. When the project scope grows without the project manager's knowledge or control, it likely reflects the project team's failure to identify important issues and resolve them appropriately. Issues affecting scope, schedule, and cost frequently evolve into scope-change requests. Project managers should put sufficient issue management controls in place to identify these significant issues, to ensure that the project team is aware of scope-change requests as they arise and can manage them appropriately.

As with all aspects of pragmatic project management, the goal of pragmatic issue management is to scale these efforts to meet the particular needs of each individual project (Figure 5-10).

For small projects, the PM can manage project issues by simply sketching out a workflow, jotting down a few roles and responsibilities, and keeping a minimal list of open issues. Large, complex projects with greater risks may require a formal, documented issue management plan. The contents of a typical issue management plan often include:

- An introduction
- An issue management process overview and workflow
- Issue management tools
- Project team roles and responsibilities
- A list of acronyms, terms, or definitions
- A sample issue management form.

Figure 5-10 Issue Management Scaling Model

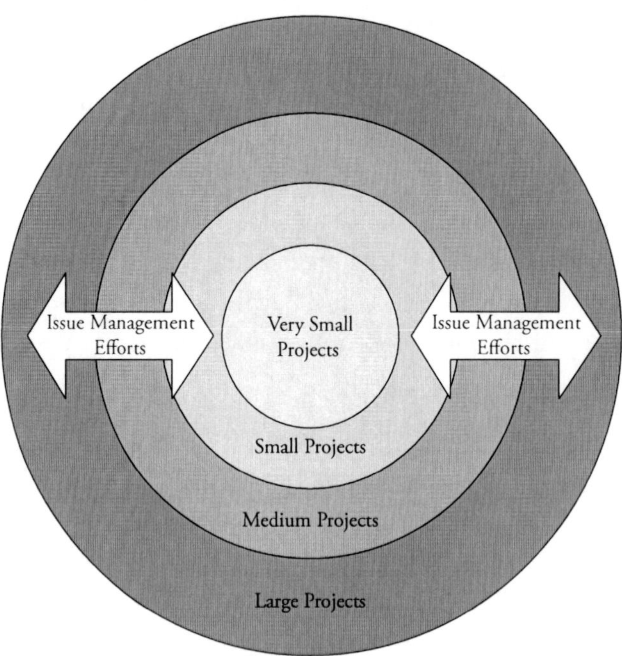

ISSUE MANAGEMENT CHECKLIST

Description	Yes	No	N/A
Issue management roles and responsibilities are defined and agreed upon with the project sponsor and project team.			
The process for issue escalation is defined and approved by the project sponsor.			
An issue tracking log is written as necessary, to include: • A unique identifying issue number • A brief description of the issue • The name of the person(s) who raised the issue • The phase(s) of the project affected by the issue • Who the issue was assigned to for resolution • Issue status (e.g., open, closed) • A brief description of how the issue was resolved • The date the issue was opened • The date the issue was closed.			

Description	Yes	No	N/A
An issue management plan is written as necessary, to include: • An introduction • An issue management process overview and workflow • Issue management tools • Project team roles and responsibilities • A list of acronyms, terms, or definitions • A sample issue management form.			
The project team and key stakeholders are informed about the issue management process for the project.			
A change control plan is developed to track changes impacting project scope, schedule, and costs as necessary for medium-sized and large projects.			
A risk management plan is developed to track risks impacting project scope, schedule, and costs as necessary for medium-sized and large projects.			
A risk management log is developed to track risks impacting project scope, schedule, and costs as necessary for medium-sized and large projects.			
Issues are addressed within reasonable time frames for high-, medium-, and low-priority issues.			
The issue tracking log is reviewed regularly with project team members at project team meetings.			
Significant issues are escalated to the project sponsor in accordance with the issue management plan.			
Key issues requiring attention from senior management are mentioned in project status reports provided to the project sponsor.			

Chapter 6

Pragmatic PM Element #5: Project Status Tracking and Reporting

Project status tracking and reporting is a key element of project success. Too many projects fail before the project team is even aware of a problem. To effectively manage and control a project, the PM must clearly understand a project's status at any point in time.

Pragmatic PM Rule #35: To effectively manage and control a project, the PM must clearly understand a project's status at any point in time.

A few years ago, I was invited into the office of one of my project sponsors. At that time, I was providing quality assurance oversight for one of the project sponsor's IT projects. We enjoyed a good rapport, so he asked if I would sit in on a status meeting he had scheduled with a project manager for another project.

I joined him in his office just before the meeting began. A few minutes later, the project manager entered the office and took a seat across the small conference table. Once the PM was settled, the project sponsor asked for a brief status report. She paused to consider a moment before responding, "We're about halfway through the project." When the sponsor asked about the budget, the PM added, "We're using some of the project's contingency budget, but we should be all right."

The project sponsor looked at me for a reaction. To me, the PM's comments raised more questions than answers. What does "halfway" mean? Halfway through the schedule? Halfway through the deliverables? Halfway through the work plan?

The statement about the project's contingency budget raised some questions as well. Was the contingency budget allocated to specific tasks in the project work plan, a specific phase of the project, or the project as a whole? How much contingency was available for the project? How were the contingency needs for the project calculated, and what percentage of the budget had been consumed?

More importantly, the information provided by the PM made it virtually impossible for the project sponsor to determine the real status of the project. After a brief discussion, the sponsor asked the PM to return to his office two days later with a detailed work plan, budget figures, and proof of task completion for every deliverable scheduled up to that point in time.

Fortunately, the project turned out to be in acceptable condition. The project team had diligently worked toward the project objectives and requirements and had accomplished most of the milestones in the project work plan. From that point on, the project sponsor was able to sufficiently track the project's progress, and the project was ultimately delivered on schedule and within budget.

Sometimes project managers bemoan writing frequent project status reports. But that attitude shows a lack of recognition of whom the project status report benefits most: the project manager. Writing a project status report forces the PM to take pause from the whirlwind of project activity and assess the project's overall condition.

Pragmatic PM Rule #36: Of all the project stakeholders, project status reporting benefits the project manager most.

The ability to understand a project's status at any point in time—including the project's status relative to its schedule, budget, and deliverables—is a key factor in project success. Project sponsors commit considerable funds and time to projects and need to feel confident that those resources are invested well.

Project status tracking and reporting is key to ensuring that both the project sponsor and the project manager have the information they need to assess the project's status at any point in time. This is why effective project status tracking and reporting is one of the five essential elements of pragmatic project management.

REPORTING PROJECT STATUS

Effective project status reporting is a key indicator of a well-managed project. Presented to the project sponsor, project team, and stakeholders, project status reports should concisely and effectively answer key questions, including:

- What is the overall condition of the project—e.g., good, bad, likely to succeed, unlikely to succeed?
- What is the status of the project's budget?
- How much work has been completed relative to the project plan?
- What has been accomplished in the most recent reporting period?
- What major tasks are coming up in the immediate future?
- What major issues needing attention from senior management are outstanding on the project?

Figure 6-1 offers a simple status report form that is easy for even the busiest PM professionals to read and digest.

Medium-sized and large projects might require reports with more detail (Figure 6-2), including earned value analysis figures, which are defined later in this chapter.

Of course, project stakeholders are interested in other information about the project, too, but the primary categories outlined in the previous status reports are the most common.

Figure 6-1 Simple Project Status Report Form

Client:			
Project Name:		**Date:**	
Tasks Completed This Period:			
Tasks Scheduled Next Period:			

Outstanding Issues:	**Point of Contact:**

Regardless of the audience, good project status reports should be timely and as brief as possible. If a report is too long and filled with tedious data, the project sponsor and other important stakeholders will be less inclined to actually read it. Senior managers have tight schedules and must process great amounts of information each day. To fit into busy schedules, project status reports and meetings must be short and to the point.

Figure 6-2 Expanded Project Status Report Form

<table>
<tr><td>Client:</td><td colspan="7"></td></tr>
<tr><td>Project Name:</td><td colspan="3"></td><td>Date:</td><td colspan="3"></td></tr>
<tr><td>Budget at Complete:</td><td></td><td>Planned Value:</td><td></td><td>Actual Value:</td><td></td><td>Earned Value:</td><td></td></tr>
<tr><td>Estimate to Complete:</td><td></td><td>Estimate at Complete:</td><td></td><td>Schedule Variance:</td><td></td><td>Cost Variance:</td><td></td></tr>
<tr><td colspan="8">Tasks Completed This Period:</td></tr>
<tr><td colspan="8"></td></tr>
<tr><td colspan="8">Tasks Scheduled Next Period:</td></tr>
<tr><td colspan="8"></td></tr>
<tr><td colspan="7">Outstanding Issues:</td><td>Point of Contact:</td></tr>
<tr><td colspan="7"></td><td></td></tr>
<tr><td colspan="7"></td><td></td></tr>
<tr><td colspan="7"></td><td></td></tr>
<tr><td colspan="7"></td><td></td></tr>
<tr><td colspan="7"></td><td></td></tr>
<tr><td colspan="7">Issues for Immediate Action:</td><td>Point of Contact:</td></tr>
<tr><td colspan="7"></td><td></td></tr>
<tr><td colspan="7"></td><td></td></tr>
<tr><td colspan="7"></td><td></td></tr>
<tr><td colspan="7"></td><td></td></tr>
</table>

When organizations invest significant funds in a project, sponsors will be eager for regular status reports providing relevant information about the project. The frequency of reporting varies. Most organizations ask for project status reports every two weeks or once a month. Giving updates more often typically becomes a redundant, recurring chore; giving reports less often than once a month typically disconnects management from the project. The PM and project sponsor should establish a reporting schedule early in the project, and they should also discuss what each status report will contain.

Pragmatic PM Rule #37: The PM and project sponsor should establish a reporting schedule early in the project, and they should also discuss what each status report will contain.

TRACKING AND CONTROLLING THE PROJECT

The project manager is responsible for tracking and controlling the project—its scope, schedule, cost, team, and so on. An awareness of project status allows the project team to anticipate the future course of the project and celebrate its accomplishments; stakeholders to plan for their involvement in the project; and project sponsors to plan for additional resources as needed.

Tracking and controlling the project means knowing the project plan; comparing the project's current status against the original plan; identifying any differences between the plan and the actual status; and making adjustments as necessary to keep the project on track.

A good project plan decomposes each project deliverable into work tasks with corresponding schedule and resource estimates. The PM can track and record the actual work, time, and resources expended for each task and compare that data to the original plan.

Consider a series of tasks in a project plan that culminate in the development of several new user interface screens for a website. When the PM checks the project status, the project team reports it has completed several tasks in the project plan. The PM can then validate that certain scheduled tasks given in the project plan have been fulfilled on time and within budget. It would be reasonable, therefore, for the PM to report to the project sponsor that the project is on track.

Pragmatic PM Rule #38: Track the completion of project tasks to confirm project progress.

OBJECTIVE AND SUBJECTIVE ASSESSMENTS

Effective status reporting incorporates both objective and subjective status measures. Objective status measures are key elements of any project status report, but so are more subjective assessments. A project manager is typically hired both for his or her skill with project management tools and techniques as well as his or her good judgment and ability to offer subjective assessments of what all the project data means. Will the project be successful? How much trouble are we in? What is our likelihood of getting back on track? If things are going well, are they likely to remain so?

Having data that validates the project is on track financially or progressing well against schedule is not enough; those indicators must be integrated with subjective feedback from the project team, contractors, and other stakeholders to form a holistic picture of the project's health. The PM must dig deeper by talking with the project team to identify exactly what the data means.

The importance of objective measures, of course, cannot be overstated. Remaining objective can be difficult for the PM: The tremendous commitment to the project by project managers could potentially bias their presentation of project status information. PMs can resist the urge to convey only positive information by using objective tools, measures, and metrics to ensure objectivity.

Performance measures are key indicators of the project's status. Project measures are often referred to as metrics and come in a variety of forms, including:

- Cost and schedule metrics
- Scope and quality metrics.

Cost and Schedule Metrics

Cost is clearly an objective metric: How much did the team plan to spend on the project? How much has the team spent thus far? What was produced as a result of expenditures? What does that mean to the project? Did the expenditures create the anticipated value of deliverables? Did the expenditures create the anticipated return on investment? These questions all address project status and can be calculated in objective terms if the project plan is complete and includes resource estimates and deliverables for each task.

Schedule data is also an objective metric and is closely related to cost metrics. The joint analysis of schedule and cost data is called earned value analysis. Earned value (EV) analysis requires a complete project plan that includes tasks, resources, work estimates, and cost estimates, and later, the actual costs of work performed. The basis of EV is the comparison of actual figures against plan estimates and the development of indices from those ratios to help predict the project's budget at completion.

For example, consider a project with an estimated cost of $1 million and an estimated schedule of 12 months. Midway through the project, deliverable reports show that 50 percent of the project work is complete at a cost of $400,000. Original project plan estimates gave a budget of $500,000 to complete half the work. Given that data, the project so far has a positive cost variance of $100,000 ($500,000 – $400,000 = $100,000 positive variance) or 20 percent ($100,000 / $500,000 = 0.2). If all other variables are fixed, the project team can use the 20 percent figure as a cost performance index and estimate a 20 percent positive variance for the entire project. This would then translate to a total project cost at completion of $800,000, 20 percent less than the original estimate of $1 million.

Earned value analysis is a powerful tool used to assess project status at a point in time and to extrapolate those figures into estimates of the project's future progress. Nevertheless, the project team must consider EV figures as only a point of departure for more holistic discussions of the project. To develop the big picture, the project team must investigate, for example, why variances occur—e.g., why the project saved $100,000 up to the halfway point in the schedule. Did the project team skip some work? If so, is the project at risk because of that omission? Or did the team come up with an innovative way of completing the work quickly? If so, can the team leverage that strategy for future benefit? Looking for explanations behind EV figures gives the project team a full picture of the project's health.

Pragmatic PM Rule #39: Earned value analysis is a key point of departure for objective assessments of project status.

Scope and Quality Metrics

An objective project status assessment analyzes project scope and quality. Project scope consists of all the project work authorized by a sponsor, including all the deliverables the project will produce. This includes the smallest project tasks as well as aggregate work packages at the top level of the project plan.

Quality equates to whether a deliverable meets specifications. If the project sponsor commissions a red, plastic deliverable, the final product should turn out red and made of plastic. If the sponsor commissions a formal study and report with specified content, the project team should conduct the study and produce a report with the specified content. If the team produces a deliverable that meets specifications within the original project time frame, all is well. If not, then the PM should investigate to find out where things went awry.

The project team can assess a project's scope and the quality of its deliverables at any time if the project plan is complete and organized by project objectives. An effective project plan is organized with objectives that trace directly to a specific aspect of the project sponsor's vision. In the same manner, project requirements trace to one or more objectives.

When the project team fulfills each project requirement, it provides some component of the final deliverable—e.g., a plan, a design, a sink installed in a washroom, a component of software. Every deliverable component should trace to the work needed to satisfy a requirement, which in turn should trace to an objective, which in turn should trace back to the project sponsor's vision. This is a simple concept, but project plans often lack this system of traceability, which can cause confusion later when tracking a project's progress.

A project manager with a solid project plan that traces the project sponsor's vision to requirements and deliverables will find it easier to evaluate project progress over time. The PM can examine the record of fulfilled work and compare it to the project plan. As the project team fulfills tasks, the PM can trace those tasks to requirements and deliverables. If the team fulfills tasks to specifications, the project is progressing as planned. If not, the PM should hold a project status meeting with the team to determine where things might have gone off course.

Pragmatic PM Rule #40: A project manager with a solid project plan that traces the project sponsor's vision to requirements and deliverables will find it easier to evaluate project progress over time.

CASE STUDY: PROVING A PROJECT'S STATUS

A few years ago, the project sponsor I worked for called me into a meeting. I was the quality assurance analyst for one of his more troubled projects, and we had established a good rapport as we worked together to bring the project back on track. When I entered his office, he asked me to take a seat and observe as a PM managing a different project provided a verbal project status report.

The PM said hello as he entered the office, and we all settled in for the meeting. When the project sponsor asked him how the project was going, he replied, "We're about halfway through. We've used only a little of the project's contingency budget, but we should be all right."

The project sponsor thanked the PM for his report. When he left the room, he asked me for my thoughts. Having heard similar project status reports before on many occasions, my response was simple: "He says the project is in good shape. Ask him to prove it."

I explained, "He should have a traceable project plan that describes all the deliverables included in the project's scope. The list of deliverables should link to specific project requirements, to project objectives, and to your vision for the project. If his team is halfway through the project, then it should have fulfilled to specifications all the work planned for completion at the halfway point in the schedule. If so, he can easily validate that his team is halfway thorough the project and that the project is in good shape. This will demonstrate that the project is in fact on track and that the team is producing high-quality deliverables according to specifications."

The project sponsor responded by asking, "Should I be concerned that he is using a portion of the contingency budget already?"

"If the contingency budget is distributed across the project's detailed project plan according to the relative risk of any specific component of the project work, and if he hasn't generated any deliverables outside the project's scope, then the use of some of that contingency budget shouldn't necessarily raise concerns. He should, however, demonstrate what value he gained from using the contingency budget—e.g., to mitigate a risk associated with a particular task."

Given this advice, the project sponsor later asked the PM to use the project plan and the list of deliverables to support his contention that the project was halfway through. The PM produced a detailed project plan that included a list of deliverables and specifications and a schedule of deliverables planned for completion halfway through the project. He showed the sponsor that his team had in fact produced the planned deliverables to specifications. The project was indeed successfully halfway through its planned schedule and was on track for completion on time.

Though the PM successfully delivered the first half of the project, he did so initially without a formal project plan. He sensed things were going relatively well, and they were. Perhaps he had organized his project team in a way that informally provided the guidance and direction necessary to keep the project on track. While this approach proved effective in producing deliverables on schedule, it did not provide quantifiable evidence of the project's progress to the project sponsor. The project sponsor felt less secure with this informal approach. He required a more robust and quantifiable status report.

Project status reporting is first and foremost a valuable tool that forces the PM to stop and assess the project's progress. The report also provides an important communications channel between the PM and the project sponsor, to exchange information and ensure that they have the same understanding of the project's status.

For some project sponsors working within informal organizational cultures with a history of successful projects, an informal, subjective report may sufficiently describe a simple, low-risk project's status. On the other hand, if a project sponsor has had a few bad project experiences, he or she may require something more substantial. Successful PMs must understand the needs and the expectations of the project sponsor and create accommodating project status reports. A good rule of thumb in any case, however, is to create a detailed project status report that reflects a thorough project plan encompassing the full project scope.

Project status reports also provide information to other stakeholders. While it is important not to burden stakeholders with an overabundance of information, a well-tailored project status report addressing specific, discrete aspects of the project that are of interest to specific stakeholders can provide great value.

Stakeholders outside of the project team are often the best evaluators of whether project deliverables meet specifications and quality standards. When the project's scope changes, or when the team or other stakeholders perceive poor quality among project deliverables, they will raise their concerns as issues. Tracking and addressing project issues carefully and expeditiously is conducive to maintaining consistent project scope and producing high-quality deliverables.

SCALING PROJECT TRACKING AND REPORTING EFFORTS

As with all efforts in pragmatic project management, the goal is to use minimum effort to ensure maximum gain for the project. Small projects typically require only a little project status tracking and reporting. Larger projects generally require more. The goal is to scale project status tracking and reporting efforts to meet the needs of each individual project (Figure 6-3).

Figure 6-3 Project Status Tracking and Reporting Scaling Model

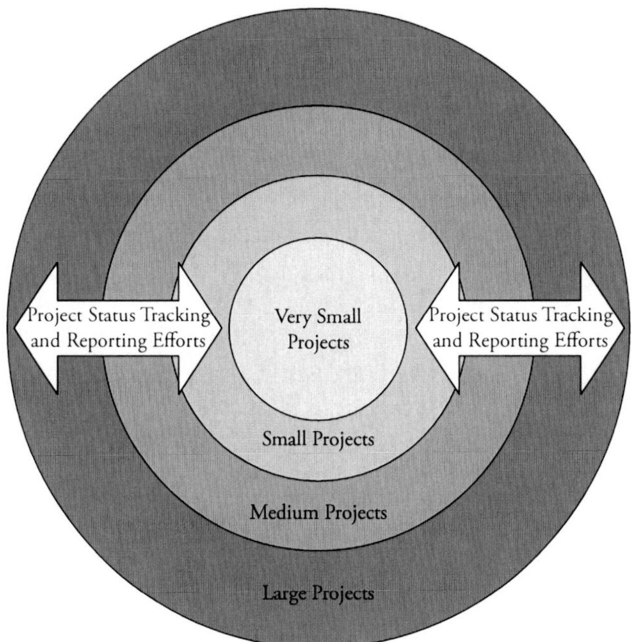

Project managers often wonder how to scale project status reporting efforts. A good rule is to create a basic project status report format for all projects, and then add more information to the format to meet the specific needs of the project and the sponsoring organization. The primary information described in each status report should include:

- The work planned for the reporting period
- The work completed during the reporting period
- The work planned for the next reporting period
- Open issues that require resolution by the project sponsor
- An update on project scope, schedule, and cost.

Project status tracking and reporting can be as simple as scratching some notes on a napkin for a very small project and discussing things with the other project team members over coffee. The project plan for small projects may include just a few tasks and deliverables. A project manager's review of those tasks and deliverables could take only minutes, but it could nevertheless result in a reasonable assessment of the project's progress compared with the plan.

Small projects might include the project sponsor as a direct member of the project team, and in such cases a meeting over coffee could sufficiently meet the sponsor's need for information. If the sponsor is not a member of the project team, a quick email or comment over lunch might sufficiently assuage any sponsor concerns or support his or her confidence that the project is progressing as planned.

A very large project's plan could include thousands of requirements and tasks, each with discrete deliverables. Assessing a complex plan against project team performance can thus be more of a challenge. In these cases, the use of automated project planning tools makes a significant difference. Many tools can produce project summaries that objectively assess schedule and cost status. Validating the quality of deliverables, however, must still be done manually by the project team.

For projects of any size or complexity, successful project status reporting depends upon the development of a detailed project plan against which the PM can compare the actual work performed and deliverables produced by the project team. Simply stated, the PM cannot determine whether the project is on course without a detailed project plan to compare with actual progress, expenses, and deliverables.

This is why larger, more complex projects may require more formal, documented project status reports. Writing detailed reports forces the PM to sit down and assess the project from a number of perspectives—both objective and subjective. Detailed status reports conveyed succinctly and effectively can reassure project sponsors and important stakeholders that the project is proceeding effectively and efficiently.

CASE STUDY: SCALING STATUS REPORTING PRACTICES

Many years ago, I was hired as a junior program manager for a large flight simulator project. The average cost for one simulator was well over $20 million, and the company I worked for was commissioned to produce

20 simulators. The customer was a government agency that had, before the project even began, expressed concern about early schedule estimates. Could the commissioned company really produce the simulators, training manuals, maintenance manuals, and spare parts on schedule?

As the new program manager on the team, it was my job to gain the customer's confidence in the simulator company's ability to deliver its products on time. I reviewed the company's prior history with the customer. In previous projects, the simulator company provided project status reports verbally at quarterly program reviews. The customer walked away from these meetings with little more than a one-page copy of an overhead slide that stated generically that the project was progressing as planned.

For a project worth hundreds of millions of dollars, this approach to status reports seemed insufficient. I was determined to provide something more substantial—a comprehensive project status report that objectively stated which tasks were planned for the reporting period; which tasks were complete; which tasks were planned in the near future; any open issues; and a basic update on project scope, schedule, and cost.

The task turned out to be quite a challenge. A full assessment of each item on the status report required a reorganization of the simulator company's internal processes, so project members could identify each discrete element of work involved to fulfill a project requirement and produce a deliverable. Project members had a general feel for this sort of thing, but detailed plans and formal reporting were lacking.

With support from senior management, we brought the PMs for each flight simulator project together and developed a standard format for the company's project plans, which included project objectives, requirements, work packages, and deliverables. Each PM returned to his or her project team and verified which deliverables identified in the standard project plan were complete.

A week later all the PMs came together again to report their findings. By combining one-page reports for each flight simulator project, we created a 20-page project status report formatted similarly to the template presented in Figure 6-2. We also created a one-page executive summary to provide to the customer at the next program review.

At the next program review, the customer was clearly frustrated with the lack of detailed project status information reported previously. My boss, the program director, provided the executive summary status report. That report contained a short assessment of the general status of the simulator projects; the projects were on schedule and on budget and had undergone no significant scope changes. The summary showed the percentage of completed work for each of the twenty simulator projects, e.g., 50 percent complete, 64 percent complete. The summary also identified several issues that required resolution by the customer for the projects to continue as planned.

The customer read and digested the report. The senior manager of the customer's team glanced over to my boss and said, "I'd like to believe that the information in this report is valid, but the information provided in the past has been pretty weak. Can you prove that the data provided in this executive summary is accurate?" My boss smiled, nodded to me, and said, "Of course." I distributed the 20-page detailed status report to each member of the customer's team. The report contained the details supporting the executive summary. The customer's senior manager smiled as he thumbed through the reports, then set them aside and said, "This is great information. What is this data based on? When you say that you have detailed project plans for each simulator, what does that mean?"

I then distributed a huge mass of paperwork consisting of each simulator project's detailed project plan. The customer requested a brief recess to review the materials, and when we reconvened, the customer's senior manager indicated his complete satisfaction with the reports. He also asked that future program reviews provide consistently formatted project status reports for each flight simulator project.

The outcome of this effort to standardize the simulator company's project status reporting was a renewed, positive relationship with the customer. The project plans were updated weekly, so that subsequent project status reports were easy to develop and support. The customer no longer requested data for assessments beyond the individual project status reports for each simulator project. The relationship prospered, and the simulator company's performance backed up its reports.

Some months later, I worked on a very small project to provide test equipment for the flight simulator's motion system. It was a two-week project that included purchasing the equipment and providing it to the customer. When two weeks had passed, I encountered the customer's representative on the production floor. He was upset because I had not provided a status report for the test equipment project. I called over to a technician who had just placed the equipment in packing containers for shipment. The technician rolled one of the crates over on a dolly for the customer to inspect. "How's this for a status report?" I asked. He nodded, smiled a little sheepishly, and we went off to have coffee together.

Both cases illustrate that even within a single company and on related projects, status reporting practices can vary according to the particular situation. In every case, however, the PM should apprise the customer of a project's status at least every few weeks. In the case of the costly flight simulators, that status update required detailed plans and analysis. For the simple, two-week project, we simply had to present the deliverable on schedule, as planned.

PROJECT STATUS TRACKING AND REPORTING CHECKLIST

Description	Yes	No	N/A
Project reporting requirements (e.g., frequency, content, audience) are developed with approval from the project sponsor.			
The project manager tracks project scope, schedule, and cost throughout the project.			
The project manager compares the project's current status against the original project plan and makes adjustments as necessary to keep the project on track.			
The project status report includes the following essential elements: • The work planned for the reporting period • The work completed during the reporting period • The work planned for the next reporting period • Open issues that require resolution by the project sponsor • An update on project scope, schedule, and cost.			
The project manager writes a project status report at least monthly.			
The project manager reviews the project status report with the project sponsor, key stakeholders, and the project team.			

Final Thoughts

People become project managers for a variety of reasons. Some are drawn to the field for an opportunity to create new things or to help others. Some become PMs as a result of certain experiences in an industry or business. Some find themselves assigned to project management responsibilities simply because their boss needed someone to fill the position.

No matter how they enter the field, PMs should know that project management is an inherently risky business, fraught with challenges, but it is also one of few professions that exists only to create or improve deliverables for clients. These combined factors are what make project management such a stimulating profession.

Thriving professionally as a project manager means learning how to manage, mitigate, and avoid many of the risks that drive so many projects to failure. Pragmatic project management is an excellent tool that can assist experienced PMs and relative novices alike. It provides a simple, straightforward approach to tailoring project management to match the unique characteristics of each project—its size, complexity, and other critical characteristics.

It can take years to gain the experience necessary to customize a methodology to meet each project's specific needs. The pragmatic project management approach will allow any project manager to successfully apply minimum project effort toward maximum project gain, without wading through years of trial and error.

Good luck with all your projects. May they all be successful!

Appendix 1

Additional Case Studies

The following case studies are drawn from real project management experiences. Examine each case and consider how you could apply the tenets of pragmatic project management to approach the situation. Recommended solutions follow each of the case studies.

CASE 1: THE IT PROJECT GONE AWRY

A state government agency has hired you to troubleshoot a floundering project. The agency has commissioned the project to produce a new IT system to support its primary business function. You arrive at the agency and report to the IT director. She suggests a meeting with several project team members and stakeholders, including the business manager who manages the end-user staff, the project manager, and the contractor hired to develop the system.

After a week of work and observation at the agency, you document the following items:

- The project will cost approximately $15 million to implement and is currently halfway through its 12-month estimated duration.
- To avoid extensive operational challenges, the new system must be online and operational before the existing system's lease expires in six months.

- The contractor submitted a well-written proposal that offered solutions to all the needs the agency described in its request for proposals. The contractor will provide the new system as a subscription service to the agency for a fixed monthly price over a period of five years.
- The PM, who is highly qualified, trained, and experienced, works for the agency IT director. Though the PM appears highly committed to the project, he seems stuck at his desk, spending long hours answering emails, filing reports, and updating requirements for the project.
- The project team rarely meets, and it has never met with system end-users. The business manager and the project manager have adjacent offices, but rarely interact with one another. The contractor reports to the business manager but does not communicate with the project manager. The contractor has never provided a formal project status report.
- The project has no written charter, project plan, communications plan, change management plan, issue management plan, or risk management plan. The PM wrote a list of requirements for the new system, but the contractor has never acknowledged or formally accepted the requirements.

What should happen immediately to put this project back on course? Sort through the evidence and describe what recommendations you would make to the agency to reorient the project toward success.

CASE 1 SOLUTION

One significant problem facing the project is its lack of formal sponsorship and a project charter. Without a sponsor and charter, the project team lacks the critical guidance and support it needs to succeed.

In situations like this, it is tempting to put the project on hold, draft a project charter, and relaunch the project. Unfortunately, that option is not feasible in this situation: The new system must be online and operational before the existing system's lease expires in six months.

Given these conditions, the first course of action you should take is to locate an agency sponsor for the project—someone who can make decisions and approve expenditures to pay for the project. Once you identify a sponsor, he or she can work with the support of the agency director to take the project reins in hand.

Once the project sponsor is confirmed, he or she can establish clear roles and responsibilities for the project team and other stakeholders. The PM can transfer to work directly for the project sponsor. The business manager can be relieved of his responsibility for contract management, which could instead be consolidated under the project manager. The business manager and IT director can be brought together to form an advisory committee reporting to the project sponsor. The agency end-users can be brought together to form a project team, and everyone can immediately resume work.

Because the project team does not have enough time to craft a full project charter, it can instead construct a detailed project plan for the remainder of the project. The project sponsor should be asked to review and approve the project plan and negotiate its terms with the contractor. The contractor should be asked to formally agree to the schedule presented in the plan.

Organizing the project team and creating a detailed project plan approved by the project sponsor and contractor should effectively bring the project back on track.

CASE 2: THE NEW HOUSE

You are a project manager for a company that specializes in new home construction. A couple commissions a single-story home of approximately 3,000 square feet with a central computer system that automates and controls many household systems, including the lighting, heating and cooling, and entertainment systems. The design shows a complex arrangement of eight small rooms clustered in a semi-circle around a large open area containing the living room, dining room, and kitchen. The project will cost an estimated $500,000 and will take ten months to finish.

The clients have commissioned homes from your company before. They typically build and sell one or two homes every five years. They are hard to please and are fond of making frequent requests that essentially modify the contract throughout construction.

Which pragmatic project management tools could you use to ensure project success in this case?

CASE 2 SOLUTION

With challenging clients like the ones identified in this case study, it is imperative that you reach early agreement on the full scope of the project and how the clients will interact with the project team. Ask the clients to sign a project charter that indicates project scope, roles and responsibilities, change-control processes, and so on. This will go a long way toward ensuring that expectations are set early in the effort.

Because the clients are likely to raise many issues throughout the project, create and maintain a detailed issue management log to record each issue and its resolution. A detailed project plan is also essential. As the clients make suggestions or request changes over the course of the project, you can assess the potential impact of those changes against the original project plan approved by the clients and the contractor.

Be sure to document each issue that evolves into a scope-change request, and make sure the clients understand how each scope-change request will impact the project's schedule and cost. Explaining the potential impact to project schedule and cost might dissuade the clients from spontaneously modifying the scope of the project.

CASE 3: THE OUT-OF-TOUCH PROJECT SPONSOR

A client asks you to advise a project manager on a $20 million healthcare project that appears to have ground to a halt. After just six months, the project is four months behind schedule. The PM is desperate: The project team is not responding to her need for support and project work because its members are busy attending to other priorities, many of which have been established by the same sponsor who commissioned the healthcare project. The project sponsor is also unavailable because she has relocated to the state capitol building to lobby for key legislation.

How do you advise the project manager? What can she do to regain the team's attention and get the project back on track?

CASE 3 SOLUTION

The project sponsor offers critical support and funds the project. In this case, a lack of communication with and support from the sponsor is posing a serious challenge to the project. You should therefore insist that the project manager arrange a meeting with the project sponsor, even if it means hiking across the city to the state capitol and asking for only a few minutes of her time.

You can explain to the project sponsor how the expensive, important healthcare project has ground to a halt and suggest several immediate responses:

- Reschedule project team members to work on several projects simultaneously. Adjust all project schedules.
- Modify the project schedule to account for the four months of schedule slip.
- Rewrite a detailed project plan to reflect these changes.
- Review the new project plan with key project stakeholders to gain their concurrence.
- Plan regular project team meetings that include the project sponsor.

With renewed access to the project sponsor and a new project plan in place, the healthcare project can resume and finish within a time frame acceptable to stakeholders.

Appendix II

The 40 Key Rules of Pragmatic Project Management

The following list combines all the rules of pragmatic project management highlighted throughout the book. Project managers can rely on these rules as a reminder of important things to consider when they manage projects.

1. All projects move through a standard, predictable project lifecycle.
2. Despite the limited amount of information available during the initial phase of the project lifecycle, the sponsoring organization should be able to make an initial estimation of the project's relative size, complexity, cost, risk, and organizational impact.
3. Projects are always more complex than they seem.
4. Taking the time to plan prior to undertaking even the smallest project increases the likelihood of success.
5. For every project, aim to conduct only a sufficient amount of advance planning needed to ensure the project's success—no more and no less.
6. Every project needs a vision: If you can't see it, you can't build it.
7. The predominant portion of a project's costs covers human resources; manage project scope, schedule, and cost estimates accordingly.
8. When all the planning is done, people execute the project work, and people get the project done.

9. The right number of project team members is the minimum number necessary to deliver the project effectively.
10. Identify human resource requirements early.
11. Shape the project approach to complement the project team's character.
12. Begin delegating work only when a good project team is in place.
13. Organizations should not hesitate to improvise and develop hybrid project team structures as needed.
14. Manage stakeholders attentively to avoid costly problems later.
15. Never be afraid to re-plan, particularly where team membership is involved.
16. Every project needs a plan.
17. Whenever possible, the project team members who will do the work should develop the corresponding portion of the project plan, with guidance and direction from the project manager.
18. The clarity of the project sponsor's vision dictates the likelihood of project success.
19. Objectives should always trace directly to the vision statement issued by the project sponsor.
20. Clear project objectives provide essential guidance throughout the project.
21. Good project objectives are always S.M.A.R.T.—specific, measurable, achievable, realistic, and time-bound.
22. Requirements should trace directly to project objectives; requirements that do not trace to any objectives are out of scope.
23. Specified and implied requirements frame the project's scope.
24. Project tasks have four critical dimensions: duration, interrelationships, resource availability, and costs.
25. Scale the project plan to meet the project's needs.
26. A small project may require only a simple sketch as a project plan; a large, complex, expensive project may require a highly detailed project plan.
27. Every project has issues; manage them or be managed *by* them.

28. Most issues are fairly easy to resolve; only a small percentage will require more work to resolve and deserve more attention.
29. The length of time it takes to resolve priority issues is a key indicator of the effectiveness of the PM and his or her team and an important predictor of project success.
30. Keep an issue tracking log to track, manage, and resolve issues efficiently.
31. Describe complex issues in an issue management form, and record less-detailed information about the issue in the issue management log.
32. When numerous issues need attention, prioritize and address the most important issues first.
33. Carefully manage issues as they arise to preclude costly scope changes late in the project lifecycle.
34. The project sponsor makes final decisions on issues impacting project scope, schedule, or cost, and issues raised by key stakeholders.
35. To effectively manage and control a project, the PM must clearly understand a project's status at any point in time.
36. Of all the project stakeholders, project status reporting benefits the project manager most.
37. The PM and project sponsor should establish a reporting schedule early in the project, and they should also discuss what each status report will contain.
38. Track the completion of project tasks to confirm project progress.
39. Earned value analysis is a key point of departure for objective assessments of project status.
40. A project manager with a solid project plan that traces the project sponsor's vision to requirements and deliverables will find it easier to evaluate project progress over time.

Recommended Reading

Goodpasture, John C. *Quantitative Methods in Project Management.* Boca Raton, FL: J. Ross Publishing, 2004.

Hilson, David, and Peter Simon. *Practical Project Risk Management: The ATOM Methodology.* Vienna, VA: Management Concepts, 2007.

Johnson, Jim. *My Life is Failure: 100 Things You Should Know to Be a Better Project Leader.* Boston: The Standish Group International, Inc., 2006.

Kliem, Ralph L. *Effective Communications for Project Management.* Boca Raton, FL: Auerbach Publications, 2008.

Kaydos, Will. *Operational Performance Measurement: Increasing Total Productivity.* New York: St. Lucie Press, 1999.

Kotter, John P. *Leading Change.* Boston: Harvard Business School Press, 1996.

Lewis, James P. *Fundamentals of Project Management, 3rd Edition.* New York: American Management Association, 2007.

Mulcahy, Rita. *PM Crash Course: A Revolutionary Guide to What Really Matters When Managing Projects.* Minnetonka, MN: RMC Publications, Inc., 2006.

Project Management Institute. *A Guide to the Project Management Body of Knowledge, 4th Edition.* Newtown Square, PA: Project Management Institute, 2008.

Rad, Parviz F., and Ginger Levin. *Metrics for Project Management: Formalized Approaches.* Vienna, VA: Management Concepts, 2006.

The Standish Group International. *CHAOS Summary 2009: The 10 Laws of CHAOS*. Boston: The Standish Group International, Inc., 2009.

Tomczyk, Catherine A. *Project Manager's Spotlight on Planning.* San Francisco: Harbor Lights Press, 2005.

Young, Ralph R. *Project Requirements: A Guide to Best Practices.* Vienna, VA: Management Concepts, 2006.

Index